Everyday
Evangelism

Other books by Randy Becton

Everyday Strength
Everyday Comfort

Everyday Evangelism

Making a Difference for Christ Where You Live

Randy Becton

Baker Books
A Division of Baker Book House Co
Grand Rapids, Michigan 49516

Published by Baker Books
a division of Baker Book House Company
P.O. Box 6287, Grand Rapids, MI 49516-6287

Printed in the United States of America

Library of Congress Cataloging-in-Publication Data

Becton, Randy.
    Everyday evangelism : making a difference for Christ where you live /
Randy Becton.
       p.   cm.
    Includes bibliographical references.
    ISBN 0-8010-5740-X (pbk.)
    1. Evangelistic work. I. Title.
BV3790.B43   1997
269'.2—dc20   96-41598

To my colaborers in evangelism
in the Herald of Truth Ministry

Over these last twenty-seven years you have prayed for, planned with, and encouraged me in every opportunity to share Jesus Christ with the lost in America, the former Soviet Union, and Mexico. You have always believed that the gospel is "the power of God for salvation" (Rom. 1:16). I'm grateful that the greatest desire of each of you is for everyone to know Christ as Savior and Lord.

Contents

Foreword

My concept of evangelism has matured in recent years. I am beginning to see evangelism as a way of life. I believe the way others see you live can lead to effective evangelism possibilities.

For the first few years Randy and I were married, our life was what most people would consider pretty normal. But when Randy became ill with cancer, our life turned into the unusual. Since that time, it seems our life together has continued getting more and more unique. I was very upset when I realized life is not like the Walton family on television. I thought my life would be like theirs, but a barrage of circumstances has often left us physically and emotionally exhausted.

We've dealt not only with Randy's illness, but with the loss of loved ones and with the constant presence of stress in relationships surrounding our immediate family.

Living, no matter how hard the circumstances, is evangelism for a Christian. That is because as Christians our lives and our responses to life are different than the world's responses. If our responses are not different, we need to examine our life to see what is at its core.

As Christians, we live in joy in spite of the circumstances of our life. Many people in crisis quit God. Or turn to bitterness. Or bail out of their marriage. But with God's grace, strength, and peace, we can cope with the crises in our lives.

Christians experience everything that everybody else experiences. The difference is that we have a joy and peace because we have the promises of God, his Spirit, and his strength to see us through every situation. This is a powerful witness if we explain to those around us that we are coping through God's power.

We don't always get to see the results of our witness, but it's so inspiring when we do. In this book Randy urges us to really pray for God to show us how we can live our lives as "everyday evangelists" to his glory.

Camilla Becton

Preface

As We Begin

On September 2, 1994, I was honored with a celebration dinner marking twenty-five years of ministry in evangelism through Herald of Truth, the oldest and largest mass media ministry in the Church of Christ. In many ways it was an amazing night for me. First, I had lived to my fiftieth year, surviving two difficult struggles with cancer. Second, the elders of my church and staff of the ministry had encouraged me to make ministry my life's work (I'm eternally grateful). Third, more than 250 friends and my family came to mark this milestone with me.

I was terribly uncomfortable with the idea of the event. I chose to go through with it because I wanted my four children to better understand what their father had been doing for a living all of their lives. I also wanted them to know the value of lifetime friendships and to see evangelism as a high priority for their own lives.

Camilla, my wife and coworker, planned the celebration using the theme "From the Country Church to Churches All Over the World." The Herald of Truth staff encouraged friends from across America to send letters for an album. Respected friends wrote many kind letters. One letter stood out for a very special reason: the author, a nurse who attended the dinner, wrote that I had been a significant factor in her conversion. She expressed appreciation for my helping her come to know the goodness of God, the grace of the Lord Jesus Christ, and the wonderful feeling of being a child of God. My role in her conversion was a revelation to me.

Her letter reminded me of a major crisis in my life in 1973—my first diagnosis with life-threatening cancer. The news came suddenly after a very short but intense illness. After surgery and one month of chemotherapy in a Houston hospital I returned to Abilene to continue extensive treatment. Over the next few months I received letters of encouragement from around the world. People pled with God to restore me. Christians wanted me to feel loved and remembered. From those many treasured messages, one stood out as unusually profound. A young mother in Kentucky wrote to remind me that I was the one who led her to Christ and assisted in her baptism. She wanted to thank me. I vaguely recalled the experience, but I was glad she remembered the day and the man.

My studies of terminal illness have led me to write several of my books. In those studies I learned that when humans approach the end of life, we focus on a few central concerns: the significance of our life, the people we love, the people who love us, and the existence and relevance of God. Does he love us and will he provide for us in the future?

A central life goal for me has been to live in such a way that people could see the gospel in what I did and said. Jesus said to his disciples, "Let your light shine before men, that they may see your good deeds and praise your Father in heaven" (Matt. 5:16).

David Gyertson in *Salt and Light* writes that Christians follow a salt and light lifestyle in a fallen world. As we do,

we are viewed by some as a preserving chemical, essential not only to hindering decay, but also sustaining life and bringing accented flavors into a tasteless society. To others, our saltiness awakens an awareness of thirst that can only be satisfied in the living waters of Christ. And for others, we become the sting in the open wounds of those fearing or even despairing the presence of such an aggravating and intrusive substance.[1]

Before I began working with Herald of Truth, I'd been in graduate school and was also preaching for a church in Nashville, Tennessee. Coming to the ministry reunited me with the work of evangelism—which was something I wanted—and established a working relationship with two outstanding evangelists, Batsell Barrett Baxter and Harold Hazelip. As a preteen I'd listened to Dr. Baxter preach and had studied under him at David Lipscomb College. I was privileged to study under Dr. Hazelip at Harding University Graduate School of Religion in Memphis, Tennessee.

In 1969, when I began working for Herald of Truth, I coordinated viewer and listener responses from radio programs and television stations across America. Some years, the number of responses exceeded forty thousand. In the beginning I answered respondents' spiritual questions, counseled them about their problems, linked them with caring Christians in a local church, or guided them in learning experiences through Christian literature and Bible correspondence courses. The goal was to do everything possible to hold up the Christian story of redemption through Christ—the gospel—so that each might choose to respond to this story by becoming a follower after God, a disciple of Jesus.

Quickly several things became clear to me about evangelism. First, evangelism is something *God* does in people's lives; we are only instruments he uses. Second, the gospel is the power of God—God really *changes* people through it. Yet when the changes occur, they vary according to the individual's readiness, and therefore, evangelism is a process, not an event. Third, churches are truly interested in people's spiritual needs. They demonstrated their willingness to do whatever they could to help people understand what God did in Christ and how each could become a part of it. Fourth, there are strengths and weaknesses in using mass media to communicate Christ to the world.

Over these last 28 years I've experienced God's gracious work in my life, my family's life, and other lives because of the ministry of evangelism. For some time, however, I've seen a trend away from evangelism as a central theme in the life of the church, and Christians seem less conscious of the lost. Evangelism has fallen on hard times. To some it's a relic. Some tell me that the church's finest hours of evangelistic opportunity and success were the '50s and '60s. Others say evangelism is still needed but is a "specialty" ministry, one of the many ministries of the church, equal in importance with all the others. A number of influential leaders think evangelism is what the church does in all its ministries.

Something more troubling is that there are thousands of Christians who strongly desire to influence their world for God; to cause their family, coworkers, and friends to see the unique beauty of Jesus Christ; to be a meaningful part of a process by which God draws people to the Christ lifted up on a cross; yet they receive little encouragement and no training to help them do what they believe God would be pleased to see them do. These people are the reason I'm writing this book.

I believe Christians can be used by God every day to impact the lives of the people around them for the glory of God. If I can, I intend to help them be God's agents of reconciliation (see 2 Cor. 5:8–21).

So many are already doing much to witness to God's character and his great redemption story. I hope to provide more encouragement. Stay with me, and let's think about the nearest thing to the heart of God—the salvation of men and women—and how he might use us in his work.

This book may be used as a study guide with a group. Questions to encourage discussion of the main points of each chapter are provided at the end of the book.

Introduction

The Great Incentive for Evangelism

Any thought that will move us a little further in the direction of being more sensitive to the lost is worth thinking about. That is my reason for sharing these thoughts. I want us to focus briefly on what I believe is the greatest evangelistic incentive in all Scripture.

Some suggest that the greatest incentive is obedience to the command of Christ to go into all the world and preach the gospel (Matt. 28:19). Truly, if we are to be faithful—we who have been bought with a price (1 Cor. 6:20)—we have to be obedient. The incentive to be obedient is a good, helpful, correct motive for evangelism. But is it the greatest motive?

Another motive for evangelism is love and concern for mankind. Jesus told us to love our neighbor as ourselves (Matt. 22:39). Love and concern for one's neighbor means seeking the highest good for him or her, not only in earthly needs but in spiritual needs as well. We may see a neighbor who is naked or hungry and refuse to clothe or feed him, instead telling him "to go in peace, be warmed and filled" (James 2:16). When we do this, we are acting as infidels and unbelievers, uncommitted to loving God by loving people (1 Tim. 5:8). It is also critical, however, to meet the spiritual needs of our neighbors—they need to be free from enslavement to sin (Rom. 6:16). The only "wages" that sin pays is "death" (Rom. 6:23). It is tragic whenever we fail to realize that a person's soul is worth more than our new cars, homes, or job promotions. Although love and concern for people is a valid and proper motive for evangelism, is it the greatest incentive for evangelism?

A third motivation that has inspired concern for the lost is the realization that lost people, those without Christ, will go to hell—an eternal state of separation and lonely punishment (Rev. 21:8). In other words, the lostness of humanity impels us to evangelize. This motive is powerful, biblical, and especially meaningful. Hell indeed is real, and those who do not know Christ are lost, helpless, and hopeless, headed for a destiny apart from God (Rom. 2:8; 2 Thess. 1:8–9). But is it the greatest incentive?

Scripture includes the above motives or incentives for evangelism. But the greatest incentive is found in Romans 1:5, where Paul describes his ministry of the gospel to all the nations as being "for the sake of his [Christ's] name." The apostle John suggests that missionaries were sent out for the sake of Christ's name (3 John v. 7). Early Christians rejoiced "to suffer dishonor for the name" (Acts 5:41 RSV). This allegiance was not a sentimental attachment to the name of Jesus but a genuine concern for his honor in the world. Christians shared the gospel with hearts filled with thanksgiving and love in response to the one who "first loved" them (1 John 4:19).

Psalm 115:1 says, "Not to us, O LORD, not to us but to your name be the glory." When Paul in Philippians 2:5–11 tells the Philippian Christians that Jesus left heaven, taking upon himself humanity—even willingly accepting the servant's role to the extent of death on a cross for our benefit—he points out that the result of his suffering servanthood and sacrificial death was that God "exalted him to the highest place and gave him the name that is above every name." God's exalting of Jesus' name had a definite purpose: so "that at the name of Jesus every knee should bow . . . and every tongue confess that Jesus Christ is Lord, to the glory of God the Father."

The greatest evangelistic incentive is to bring glory to God (Ps. 51:12–15; John 15:8). Paul envisioned the possibility that people from every tribe and every language would bow their knee and confess the name of Jesus, thereby giving glory to God (Phil. 2:10–11). Every Christian who participates in the evangelistic vision of Paul can envision the people on a thousand hills bowing their knees to Jesus as Lord, and each Christian works to accomplish this evangelistic vision.

In the Old Testament God is often described as a jealous God: "I, the LORD your God, am a jealous God" (Deut. 5:9; 6:15). "I . . . will be jealous for my holy name" (Ezek. 39:25 KJV). Jealousy is an intolerance of rivals. Israel was God's bride (Jer. 2:32), and throughout Old Testament history God had a covenant with Israel—a marriage covenant (Deut. 7:12). God's quarrel with his people was that they continually violated the covenant, committing spiritual adultery through idolatry (Deut. 29:25; Jer. 13:27). Because God is the only true and living God, because he is the sole creator and sustainer of humanity, because he is the Lord of everyone, he has the exclusive right to the exclusive worship of everyone (Exod. 34:14). In Isaiah 45, God continually reminds his people:

> I am the Lord, and there is no other,
> besides me there is no God. . . .
> a righteous God and a Savior;
> there is none besides me.
> Turn to me and be saved,
> all the ends of the earth!
> For I am God, and there is no other.
> By myself I have sworn. . . .
> To me every knee shall bow,
> every tongue shall swear.
>
> Isaiah 45:5, 21–23 RSV

Jesus emphasized his Father's right to the exclusive worship of each person when he said: "You shall worship the Lord your God and him only shall you serve" (Matt. 4:10 RSV). You and I, as God's people, share God's jealousy over those who do not give him the glory due his name. Paul shared God's jealousy when he went into Athens. The Scripture says Paul's spirit was "provoked within him" when he saw that the city "was full of idols" (Acts 17:16). He longed for them to know and honor the only God (Acts 17:23–27).

Paul describes converts in an interesting way. We think of converts in terms of the salvation that is brought to the individual believer and its great value. One soul is worth more than the whole world. True. But Paul adds another idea when he says: "[I am] a minister of Christ Jesus to the Gentiles in the priestly service of the gospel of God, so that the offering of the Gentiles may be acceptable" (Rom. 15:16 RSV).

Paul says we offer converts to God as worship to him, bringing him glory. That is the supreme reason why we long to convert people to Christ—to bring glory to God.

The greatest evangelistic incentive is the glory of God. The supreme reason why God desires "all men to be saved and to come to a knowledge of the truth" is, according to 1 Timothy 2:5–6, "there is one God and one mediator between God and men, the man Christ Jesus, who gave himself as a ransom for all."

We must present the gospel of Christ to all so that we may "bring many sons to glory" (Heb. 2:10). God offers all people adoption through the cross (John 1:12; Rom. 8:14–15). But to accept such adoption, people must renounce their revolt against the authority of God and their bid for life independent of him (Eph. 1:5; 2:1–3). Paul in 2 Cor. 5:18–21 says that God reconciled us to himself through Christ and gave us the ministry of reconciliation. Out of our response of gratitude for God's grace, we are privileged to beseech people on behalf of Christ to be reconciled to God.

We participate in the nature of God when we seek for the lost because above all else our God is a seeking, searching, saving God (Luke 15). We have been privileged to be called his children. Paul says, "if children, then heirs" (Rom. 8:17 RSV). May I add, if children, then joint participants in the mission to "bring many sons to glory." What better way to glorify God? We say, with Paul, "To him be the glory forever! Amen" (Rom. 11:36).

1

Telling the Story

Anyone who gives a cup of water in Christ's name
tells the story.

William Barry

Jesus asks: "Who do you say that I am?" To some, Jesus
is the Son of God, the promised Savior, the Christ. To others, he is just a man who inspired, through his teachings
and good life, the Christian religion. And to others, he's a
myth, an invention of the church. The December 1994
issue of *Life* magazine pictures Jesus on the cover and asks,
"Who was he?" *Life*'s editors then set out to interview "emi-
nent" thinkers—scholars, historians, theologians, ministers, and even an atheist—to find out why Jesus matters so
much today. Peter Bien, professor of English at Dartmouth
College, says, "I don't think we know who Jesus was." The

atheist Jon Murray adds, "There was no such person in the history of the world as Jesus Christ."[1]

Michael Horton, editor of *The Agony of Deceit,* writes:

> The whole Christian faith rests on a scheme of redemption. It's not about men and women climbing up to God, it's about God descending to save a rebel race. God appeared in the flesh, coming down to us, because we had proved we couldn't save ourselves.[2]

The Bible instructs: "Give him the name Jesus, because he will save his people from their sins" (Matt. 1:21) and announces: "Today in the town of David a Savior has been born to you; he is Christ the Lord" (Luke 2:11). Who Jesus is and what he did is what evangelism is all about.

William Willimon, one of my favorite authors, calls Christ's coming to earth "the intrusive word," and states that "evangelism is a gracious . . . byproduct of the intrusions of God." God has, because of his lovingkindness, come to us in Jesus Christ, reconciling the world to himself as Paul says, and has given us both the message and the work of reconciliation (2 Cor. 5:18–21). As Willimon says, each Christian then is "called to sign, signal, and witness to the graciousness of God in a world dying for lack of salvation."[3]

The Power of *Your* Story

Leighton Ford spends his life traveling around the globe assisting everyday Christian believers with their desire to tell others about God. He believes if you and I have become a part of the story of God, then we have a story to tell those around us. He says, "Evangelism isn't about formulas and programs. It's about what God has done in our lives . . . the result of God's story intersecting with our story. He is the evangelist—not us."[4] Our story is not where we were born, who our parents were, what we do for a living, and so on. Our *real* story is how our stories have met God's redemption story, what God has done to transform us from lives of hopeless self service to having a place in his family. James Packer says, "A Christian is a person who has God as father," building on 1 John 3:1: "How great is the love the Father has lavished on us, that we should be called children of God!" Paul told the Corinthians that the gospel story begins with "Christ died for our sins" and that this truth changes us (see 1 Cor. 15:1–3).

During my university training, our professors stressed the importance of ministers building a strong library and often advised, if we were faced with choosing between a nice meal in an upscale restaurant or buying a good book, to "go hungry for the Lord." One of the first "essential" books was Milligen's *Scheme of Redemption,* a classic of the American restoration movement. Milligen saw a unifying theme to all sixty-six books of the Bible and said that the Bible is really one great story telling what God in love did to save people. Being a Christian means that this is your story.

I grew up in Nashville, Tennessee, and I've always taken a certain pride in the "Athens of the South." To understand me you have to know something about my being a Southerner. But my real identity is as a Christian. I became a Christian early in life because different individuals told me the story and lived the gospel before me in Woodbine, South Nashville, the Hillsboro Church of Christ, the Wingate Church of Christ, the Short Mountain Youth Camp, and other places.

They told me the "old, old story of Jesus and his love" in ways that made me desire to make this my story, to make

"Christian" my name. My looks, name, family, and traditions were given to me by others. But God's grace alone gave me the privilege to be his son and to have a place in his family. I grew up singing the Christian hymn, "This is my story, this is my song, praising my Savior all the day long"—a testimony to my story of blessed assurance in Jesus Christ. Have I got a story to tell! And you do too!

As we approach the twenty-first century many people are living by other stories. So "evangelism is a matter of addressing those who live by narratives other than the gospel."[5] Christians are mistaken if they believe that these people don't need to hear our story or that telling them the story requires arm-twisting and high-pressure tactics. The lost absolutely need to hear the gospel. Then, why not use the oldest, purest, most natural way to tell it—using opportunities that come in relationships? Will this method be effective? Will it win? I assure you it will meet with the same response that Paul, Peter, and the early Christians experienced: "some of them sneered, but others said, 'We want to hear you again on this subject.' . . . A few men became followers . . ." (Acts 17:32–34).

Lost people are captured by many lies. They live under the dominion of the enemy. That's why they are lost. Paul says they are spiritually dead and alienated from God. He adds that they are by nature hostile to God and estranged from him (see Ephesians 2:1–3).

Reconciliation involves bringing sinful humanity out of alienation into a state of peace and harmony with God. Jesus the reconciler heals the separation and brokenness created by sin and restores the relationship between God and us. Reconciliation is an act God performed to deliver us from estrangement. He did it through the cross; the cross that offends the sensitivities of sinful people was necessary because we had rejected God (Rom. 5:12–19; 8:17).[6]

Sin is real and mars God's image in people. To speak of Jesus' death, burial, and resurrection will be "foolishness to those who are perishing" today as it was in Paul's Corinth (see 1 Cor. 1:18). This is important when some insist on measuring success in numbers rather than in our faithfulness in telling the story. Jesus said, "The Son of man must be lifted up, that everyone who believes in him may have eternal life" (John 3:14–15). Our job, then, is to lift him up and so begin the process of reconciliation.

Fear of Failure

Let me tell two stories. In 1966 I spent a week in Gaffney, South Carolina, assisting an evangelist in a five-night gospel outreach. My job was to visit a section of Gaffney door-to-door and invite people to come to the evening services. If the opportunity arose, I spoke with people about Jesus. One day I had the good fortune to find a fine young man my own age who was open and searching for meaning in his life. He encouraged me to tell him the story of what God has done to save people. Jim listened intently and asked good questions. I grew expectant. I thought, *This is going well.* After two hours the story had been told. The time seemed right to ask if Jim desired to make the story his personal story. He didn't. No objections. No explanations. I was crushed and demoralized. I felt like a failure.

That was a long time ago, and now I know more about the process of evangelism. I know that I did exactly what God wanted me to do. He was pleased. The experience was successful in that I did my part well. Perhaps Jim said yes

later, God knows. But I had not failed. I simply hadn't fulfilled my unrealistic expectations.

A second story: In Glasgow, Scotland, in 1964 I received
a stunning invitation to visit in the home of a man who
had just been released from prison after serving a four-year
term for a crime he never specified but was probably rob-
bery. His wife and two sons had waited patiently for him
and had warmly begun a new chapter of their life with him.
I was welcomed by them because they were fascinated by
Americans, especially Americans who would go "on holi-
day" to talk to people about their faith. They knew no one
personally whose religious faith formed his or her life's priorities. After tea and pastries they asked me to tell them
about my faith. So off I went on the greatest story ever told.
As I recall, we visited for three hours. I missed the eleven
o'clock bus back to the hotel from their apartment. The
man offered to walk me back, and so we walked the streets
of Glasgow until after midnight. He warmly thanked me.
But there was no movement of his heart to embrace the
story as his story. We had other visits, but there was no spark
of commitment. I was downcast. *What's wrong with me?
Why am I not more persuasive? Where could I go to learn to
"close the sale"?* My heart ached over this family.

Was this another failure? I believe God directed my visit
to that dear family. His Word was truthfully and lovingly
presented. I had prayed fervently. Could it be that God
accomplished his purpose for that night? I had fulfilled my
role in his process of evangelism; the rest was up to him.

I tell the two stories not because they are pleasant. They
are painful. Yet they point out what I believe is a major
obstacle to telling the story today: fear of failure. We fear
rejection, hostility, loss of face. Our self-respect and dignity can handle very little rejection. Bill Bright, a name vir-

tually synonymous with evangelism, is president of Campus Crusade for Christ and wrote *Witnessing without Fear.* He believes fear of personal rejection paralyzes Christians and limits their speaking to non-Christians about Jesus. This may explain our great interest in "just living for Christ and letting people see our actions." Some refer to it as *service* evangelism. It minimizes rejection.

Bill Bright says, "It hurts . . . when we've reached out in genuine love and we see the person refuse the greatest gift ever offered to mankind, God's son. Compassion for the lost does not come without tears."[7]

I'm reminded of a visit my wife, Camilla, and I had with the director of the Boys Club of Brownsville, New York, in the late sixties. We were considering moving from a church in Nashville to Brownsville to direct an inner-city ministry in a crime-ridden, lower socioeconomic area of New York. Picture this: he, a tall, athletic Black young man, well educated, a straight talking no-nonsense leader in the community, caring, and articulate; me, a tall, athletic Southern White young man, a minister, caring and naive. Ralph began our interview by complimenting me on my desire to help people. He then reminded me that many so-called "Christian" people had exploited the poor and really made their situations more hopeless. He offered this advice: "Randy, if you move here you'll need to roll up your sleeves and serve the people, and *keep your mouth shut.* After you have demonstrated Christianity for a few years, then it will be appropriate for you to say something about Jesus. But not until then!" I appreciated his candor. I partially understand his perspective. Yet how could I be faithful to the story and do what he suggested? Jesus acted redemptively while at the same time speaking the words of the kingdom of God. It's not one or the other. Actions *and* words are necessary. Acts begins with Luke saying he "wrote about all that Jesus began to do and to teach until the day he was taken up to heaven"(Acts 1:1–2).

Steve Sjogren reminds us that few unchurched people are looking for a church. What they are looking for is relief from their pain. Steve teaches compassionate outreach to people: "If we can come to understand what that pain is, think creatively about ways to relieve it, and then demonstrate unconditional love, we will have come a long way toward the goal of reconciling those people to God."[8]

He assumes if you love enough, identify enough, relieve enough, then people will naturally want God to rule in their lives. This thinking appeals, but it's not always the case. His conclusion is, "Valued people will become redeemed people when we have earned their trust and persuaded them, through both our words and deeds, that the gospel really is the Good News that it claims to be, that it is relevant to their lives."[9]

Valued people often become more open to considering the gospel, but we must remember that becoming redeemed is to accept the scandal of the cross and to submit your rebellious will to God. Steve is right to show that people who experience Christian compassion catch a true glimpse of God's love. Whether they respond and embrace it is another matter. We need to understand this truth without being discouraged.

There is a place for Christian service in evangelism—a very important place. People often experience the love of God for the first time through service evangelism. We must, however, be certain that Jesus' name is connected to the service. We must not leave out the name of the one who brings hope and a new day to our lives. The cup of cold water is to be given in the name of Jesus. If we give the cup of cold water in Jesus' name, we will not fail. Did Jesus fail with the rich young ruler, with Judas, with the multitudes? Near the end of his life he prayed, "I brought glory to you here on earth by doing everything you told me to" (John 17:4 LB).

The only failure we need fear is the failure to tell and live the story. Then we must leave it to God, for unless God works in people's hearts, nothing happens.

Read again Jesus' story of the sower in Matthew 13:3–8. Four possible results of sowing the seed are given. I'm convinced there is no wasted telling of the story. For sure, God hears it every time. Like a Persian rug, we are looking at only one side. God sees both sides. He knows the design being woven. To leave the results up to God allows us to focus on what we are to do.

God Converts People

The Bible says the Spirit of God convicts men and women of sin when the gospel is spoken (John 16:8–11). My friend William Abraham points out that God initiates the process of conversion in people's lives and that Christians are useful to God in his process.[10]

The great evangelist John Wesley believed that God is busy working in people's lives from the beginning. He looked back on his own life and saw many evidences of "an unseen hand" lovingly guiding him toward God. Each of us can see the same evidences, leading to that point in our lives where we responded to God's love and accepted his saving grace in baptism. Francis Thompson's *Hound of Heaven* speaks of God's long pursuit of us.

I've counseled many sad Christians in their time of grief after they bury a parent, and I listen to the guilt they feel

for never having helped their loved one come to Christ.
Some of their guilt is unnecessary (although the sadness is
fully understandable) because we are not God's *only* influence in a person's life. There have been many proddings,
encouragements, and displays of love God has brought into
our loved one's life. It may be that we didn't fully maximize
our time of opportunity, but we were one of a long line of
influences that were rejected.

What I'm emphasizing is that God's initiative *precedes*
our response, and we must remember this. When we tell
the story, God has already been at work before we arrive.
We are not telling a story we created. God is constantly
working on behalf of his redemptive love.

2

A Passion for Evangelism

There is something wrong with a Christian who does not have a passion for evangelism.

J. I. Packer

Where should evangelism be done? In church? At the office? Under an evangelistic tent? If evangelism is "the normal expression of the Christian experience," then it must be a part of our everyday lives.

Defining Evangelism

Elton Trueblood, author of *The Incendiary Fellowship*, believes "evangelism occurs when people are so enkindled by contact with the central fire of Christ that they, in turn, set others on fire." Trueblood thinks evangelism is a way of viewing people, a way of conversation, a way of behavior, a lifestyle. This truth frees us to be light, salt, and leaven in our homes, workplaces, and communities. We'll move beyond the mistaken idea that "the focal point of the local church's corporate evangelistic effort is the eleven o'clock worship on Sunday morning."[1]

The picture I see in Acts 8 is the church scattering everywhere telling the story of what God had done. Each Christian, in the normal flow of everyday living, sought to demonstrate the way of the cross by what he did; and he spoke of a crucified and risen Savior and Lord, Jesus Christ. "The Christian man or woman, redeemed by Jesus Christ and filled with the Holy Spirit, must make the task of witnessing to his or her faith the magnificent obsession of life. If a person has been died for, then little else matters as much."[2] We know the joy of release from the guilt and power of sin. Nothing brings us greater satisfaction than to testify about the love of God. Earl Hunt says, "To know the joy of belonging to God is to wish someone else to know it. To have Christ is to desire to share him with others . . . [to lead] another for whom you have concern into the light that has broken up your own darkness."[3]

But isn't evangelism more than a wish, a desire, to lead others? Isn't it a life and a ministry that show that God's story of redemptive love has become one's own story? It is intentionally living so that God uses our words and actions in his evangelistic work in people's lives. We are vessels for heaven's use.

Michael Green teaches evangelism at Regent College in Vancouver, British Columbia. His *Evangelism through the*

Local Church is a comprehensive guide to evangelism. In it he defines three types of evangelism:

1. a spontaneous, continuous speaking
2. one beggar telling another beggar where to get bread
3. a presentation of Jesus Christ in the power of the Holy Spirit so that people will put their trust in God through him, accept him as their Savior, and serve him as their King in the fellowship of his church

Green likes the third description best and says, "The earliest Christians were always at it: in the shops and the streets, in the laundries and on the seashore."[4]

Green thinks we don't do what the early Christians did because

We think it's not our business.
We don't have a firsthand faith.
We're not sure of our salvation.
We're not close to the Lord.
We're fearful.
We're ignorant.
We're culturally isolated.

There are elements of truth in his observations; however, perhaps we simply need to be shown *how* to live an evangelistic lifestyle. Rather than feeling guilty, we need to dispel our fears and misconceptions about witnessing.

We should not be intimidated by the word *witness*. In the Bible the word translated *witness* is the root for the word *martyr*. It means we have seen and heard something (namely the love of God in Christ) that has totally changed our life and so we are willing to tell about it—when it's well received and even when it's not. We have been transformed so that all we do is done *in the name of Christ.* Doing things in Jesus' name means, as William Willimon says, "Jesus blessed ordinary people so that they might go forth to be a blessing for others . . . and show forth the good news in word and deed" (Luke 10:1–22).[5]

People with the Passion

Frances Willard led the Women's Christian Temperance Union in the late 1890s because she knew God's business is helping people in his name. She believed faith in Jesus Christ should lead one to help men, women, and children whose lives were made miserable by alcohol.

William and Catherine Booth believed the gospel should be shared with the poor in England in the 1850s, and their work led to the founding of the Salvation Army. These people were convinced that the gospel is to be shared in word and action.

I attended a wedding, conducted by my good friend Dr. Charles Siburt, of two university graduates who have a strong allegiance to Christ. The design, content, and style of the wedding conveyed the intention to display the wisdom of God, the glory of God, and the kindness of God in giving humans the gift of marriage. In the audience that day were relatively few unbelievers, yet they experienced an evangelistic outreach of the gospel by being there.

To my knowledge Dr. Siburt speaks only rarely in evangelistic campaigns. Yet in most of his activities that serve people he speaks of the story of what God has brought about in Christ. For several years he chaired the board of the local hospice. In staff development, board policy creation, and interpersonal contacts he has served people with redemptive intent. His evangelistic outreach is a way of seeing, speaking, and acting.

During my training at David Lipscomb University I had the privilege to drive out to a small country church on Sundays near Manchester, Tennessee, to preach morning and evening services. The most unforgettable character in that sixty-member church was brother Lynch, a snaggletoothed sixty-five-year-old former bootlegger who taught the older adult Sunday school class. He was a gracious, gentle man and soon took me under his wing and devoted himself to encouraging "the young minister." He told me stories about his wild days that curled the hair on the back of my neck, but he always told them with a sad, regretful tone that helped me understand why "Amazing Grace" was his favorite hymn. His second favorite was "Love Lifted Me." He had fought "the revenuers," cheated many fellow bootleggers, and had embittered his wife through years of neglect. Brother Lynch often said, "Randy, I've done much wrong, many evil deeds, and don't deserve God's kindness at all. But I have been changed and I'm trying to show my gratitude by helping other old moonshiners to see that God loves them and they are welcome in his house."

He suffered from bad health. He lived in a shack in the country. Yet he arose each day with energy, whistled hymns through those gapped teeth, and sought to help everyone he could "in the name of the Lord." He couldn't help it. A grateful heart led him on. What about you? How far have you come in acknowledging that without God you would be lost? Your lifestyle reflects your appreciation level.

William Willimon says in *The Gospel for the Man Who Has Everything* that a past of deprivation and wild living is not required for us to have a powerful redemption story to tell. However, sometimes those of us who for years may have had blessings poured over our heads are ungrateful. We have never given God the praise for what we have and how blessed we are. We are guilty of practical atheism, and yet "Amazing Grace" is our song too. Those who believe they have always been Christians because they have had no profound change from a life of rebellion to a life of faith have missed the radical change God brings about when one comes to Christ. Our stories have changed. We used to live as if God didn't exist. Now we live with gratitude for what he has done for us. Only a grateful heart will yield a passion for evangelism that is seen in a life devoted to being used by God to bring others to himself.

Willimon shows the need for gratitude:

> We follow Jesus, not because it was our idea, or because we were searching for something in our lives, or because we made a study of all the world's great religions and decided that Christianity is the best. We are here, because we have been encountered, assaulted, intruded upon. Jesus has made us his own.[6]

He is *not* saying we had no choice. He *is* saying God gave us the opportunity, provided the occasion, for our salvation. That's why gratitude for what *he* has done is so important. Jesus told his disciples, "You did not choose me, but I chose you . . . to go and bear fruit—fruit that will last" (John 15:16). Jesus also said: "No one can come to me unless the Father who sent me draws him. . . . They will all be taught by God. Everyone who listens to the Father and learns from him comes to me" (John 6:44–45).

Everyone is invited, but God draws us. We decide, and it's a life or death decision. "God penetrates wherever he is allowed to enter."[7]

3

The World
We Live In

To wish to share one's knowledge of the Savior with others is natural, and to do so is felt as a privilege, just as it is seen to be a duty, a central element in neighbor love.

J. I. Packer

We must sketch a realistic picture of our world. First, however, remember Jesus' words. Following his resurrection Jesus promised his followers:

All authority in heaven and on earth has been given to me. Therefore go and make disciples of all nations, baptizing them in the name of the Father and of the Son

and of the Holy Spirit, and teaching them to obey everything I have commanded you. And surely I am with you
always, to the very end of the age.

Matthew 28:18–20

In the last thirty months I've spent significant periods of
time in Washington, D.C., where it's difficult to remember
that Jesus has all the authority. Not everyone there acknowl-
edges this fact! It's easy to see that many think power is up
for grabs, available to whoever is quickest and smartest.
Many leave the impression that their lives are self-created,
a matter of their choosing their own story, their own destiny. They appear uninterested in God's intentions for people. We're sent to them with the story that will turn their
lives upside down, bring them abundant life. As we go Jesus
whispers, "I am with you."

A World Without

In modern America everyone wants to be an individual,
to think for oneself, to make one's own decisions and be
answerable to no one. We frantically search for answers to
loneliness, fragmentation, alienation. We protect our freedom at all costs. But we don't understand that true freedom is the willingness to listen to the truth that *Jesus is Lord*
and follow along behind him. Alvin Toffler in *Future Shock*
confessed: "On the edge of a new millennium, on the brink
of a new stage in human development, we are racing blindly
into the future. But where do we want to go?"[1]
We're living in a world where people increasingly believe
in something other than a living, personal God. Will
Durant, the historian, says "the greatest question of our
time is not communism versus individualism, not Europe

versus America, not even the East versus the West; it is whether men can live without God."[2]

The great Russian author Alexandr Solzhenitsyn says that when the history of our time is written it will record that man has forgotten God. Not only is ours a world largely without faith in God, but also it's a world without much love (but with a lot of sex), without fulfillment, truth, or hope. Os Guinness paints the biblical view of the world as God's gift to us but the devil's gauntlet, a world with a spirit that stands against God. We who are reconciled to God speak to a world that is alienated, estranged from God. We take our signals from the God who *so loved the world* that he gave his Son. We long for the day when "the kingdom of the world has become the kingdom of our Lord and of his Christ, and he will reign for ever and ever" (Rev. 11:15). We, as children of God, have a great stake in protecting our Father's honor in his world.

The Psalmist in Psalm 100 says we must remember that we didn't make him. He made us. In Genesis 1 we are told that we're made in "his image." He is the Creator; we are his creation. He is our source, our sustenance, and whatever future life we have relates to him. My firm conviction is that we are to gratefully acknowledge that our purpose in living is to bring him honor and glory.

Myron Augsburger pleads for us to integrate "evangelism into every hour of the week, so that Christ is carried into people's lives, into our work, play and socializing" so that faith in Christ becomes an option for as many as we can influence.[3]

Let's not assume that people don't want to hear the gospel. John Bright says, "The yearning of people around us is really a desire to enjoy the fruits of the Kingdom of God. We Christians should feel as deeply as possible the reality of these longings."[4] God is already at work in so many lives;

let's work with him by telling his story. Only his Word will transform this world.

Evangelizing Our Modern Culture

Sociologist Hervé Carrier of the Gregorian University in Rome has made a special study of modern culture. He observes that "announcing Jesus Christ to modern minds calls for a profound revision of traditional methods of evangalization."[5]

He's convinced that people of "modern sensibilities and mentalities" won't adopt Christian values until Christians revitalize their own faith. He poses two questions: How can the church of Christ make itself understood by the modern spirit, so proud of its achievements and at the same time so uneasy for the future of the human family; and who is Jesus Christ for the men and women of today?[6]

He believes the impact of modern science and technology, the high mobility of people today, the emphasis on individualism, the growth of the media, and the fact that so many people have already rejected Christianity—so much so that many refer to post-Christian America—all of this demands reframing the Christian message, without changing the content.

No matter how modern, how urban, how technologically advanced, the heart of man remains the same—alienated from God. The good news is still our critical need. We can trust that the God who made us is the only one who can quench the hunger in our souls.

We can be more effective in telling the story when we understand the other stories people live by. Their worldviews provide entry points for God's story.

George Hunter, author of *How to Reach Secular People,*
and dean of the School of Evangelism and Church Growth
at Asbury Seminary in Kentucky, conducted more than
one thousand face-to-face interviews with persons who
came to faith in Jesus from a secular worldview. He dem-
onstrates the advantages of understanding people's worldviews when talking with them about things that matter.[7]
Michael Green tells how to witness to people entrenched
in New Age schools of thought, such as humanism, nar-
cissism, agnosticism, and pragmatism. He recommends a
caring, respectful identification with where they are, followed by the telling of the story of Jesus' death for our sins,
burial, and resurrection.[8]

In his book *How Will They Hear if We Don't Listen?*
Ronald Johnson underscores the absolute necessity of
genuine empathy for and intent listening to individuals
as prerequisites for their being able to hear the good news
of Christ from us. In a hurry-up world, we've become
accustomed to snap judgments and hasty conclusions.
We can begin giving redemptive words to more people if
we'll close our mouth when necessary. Johnson says, "We
can actually learn to tell the gospel to others more effectively as we practice the art of care through listening to
them."[9]

To understand modern worldviews you don't have to be
a specialist or scholar. In the first century, "Christ's church—
a body assembled from nothing but a ragtag bunch of
nobodies"—was used by God to change the world by telling
of a risen Lord.[10] Anyone can care, listen, and share.

Taking our signals from God, we offer the gospel to an
alienated world through our caring evangelism. William
McKay, as he focuses on empathy, describes what caring
evangelism does in the world:

Caring evangelism communicates, through word and deed, the Good News about Jesus Christ to Christians and non-Christians in a process-oriented, other-centered way so that others discover their need for a Savior, receive the forgiveness and new life that God gives in Jesus, and respond to God's love faithfully.[11]

In caring evangelism people are free to respond to the story and are not argued into the kingdom of God. We remember that the Holy Spirit convicts people of sin. The Word of God births their faith. God transforms people's lives. Since 1969 Herald of Truth Ministry has utilized this approach. And since 1978 Camilla and I have directed the National Caring Cancer Ministry using many of these principles. *All* Christians can participate in caring evangelism. As the song reminds us:

> If you cannot sing like angels,
> If you cannot preach like Paul,
> You can tell the love of Jesus,
> And say He died for all.

Certainly our world needs to hear this message and each disciple can do his or her part in God's reconciling work through the gospel.

4

Ordinary Christian Evangelists

Healthy and hopeful groups are naturally evangelistic.

Gareth Icenogle

Only my family knows the powerful influence Nellie
Hertzka Morehead had in my life. Her single-minded devo-
tion to bringing God honor in the world led her to begin
a children's orphanage in Japan from 1925–1930 and then
return to the States to help her husband run a Christian
bookstore for almost fifty years. But her quiet, shy demeanor
was easily misunderstood. She lacked nothing in drive and
determination to do anything she could to help people
understand and respond to God's love.

She never drove a car. Therefore, the bus drivers who transported her were an important part of her world, and she took special notice of them. They became part of her strategy for outreach. Also, there were her beauty shop friends whom she visited every two weeks for her shampoo and set (the only "luxury" I ever saw her give herself). Then there were her trash collectors. And her mailman. And her neighbors on three sides of her house. Then her sister's children (Nellie had none). There were the people she read about or heard about in the city who had suffered tragedies, to whom she ministered through cards and literature. She would travel to the county hospital and visit room by room those who were longtime residents, making friends with the ones most willing. She would arrange a day each month to visit the women's prison, ask the matron on duty who would enjoy a visit, and then meet and chat with that one, asking about her needs and the welfare of her family.

This quiet Jewish Christian never talked much about this caring evangelistic lifestyle, but from a distance I watched her make these rounds for more than twenty-five years. What a fascinating Christian! Always helping, serving, giving because she believed God was pleased. Occasionally someone asked her about God. She would respond by offering to read the Bible—without commentary—with the person. Reading from the Gospels, either Luke or John, she wanted people to become acquainted with Jesus, his claims, his way with people, his death, burial, and resurrection. After many months a prisoner or a patient would become a Christian. Nellie seemed very pleased but said little. She didn't view herself as unusual or special. She thought all Christians did things like that. No one taught her about outreach or pleaded with her to care for others. To my knowledge she knew little about "spheres of influence."

Nellie Hertzka Morehead was grateful for God's story. She wanted to tell it to others.

Evangelism today is being done by thousands of Nellies. Perhaps by knowing about a few, you and I will "go and do likewise."

Jon, a friend of mine in his thirties, has carefully structured his life around living the story and speaking the story. He made an evangelistic lifestyle a priority for himself. First, he prayed that he would come to see people the way the Father sees them. He requested strength and wisdom to live among his family, friends, neighbors, and strangers with a servant heart and with no reluctance to speak God's name or credit God for the good things in his life. Whenever possible he read material that described the worldview of his peers, Baby Boomers or Baby Busters (sometimes called yuppies). He became familiar with the analysis of the human life cycle, which describes the events and transitions that occur from one's birth to one's death.

Then he attempted to form meaningful relationships with a selected number of people in his life. With his wife he began to learn how to lead an evangelistic Bible study. Over the last fifteen years he and his wife have seen several people come to the Lord. Yet he refrained from becoming the "deacon in charge of personal evangelism." He wrote no books on the subject. He wanted this emphasis to be a natural part of his discipleship. Some who have seen his quiet, determined course of action have imitated him from a grateful heart.

Kenneth Hemphill, the president of Southwestern Seminary in Fort Worth, tells of putting his six-year-old daughter to bed one night by reading John 3:16 to her and helping her memorize it. Finally, she got it perfect. Ken says, "She was thrilled; her crystal blue eyes leaped for joy. Then she looked straight into my eyes and repeated a single phrase, 'Do not perish, Daddy. Do not perish.'"[1] He had never seen the stark truth that apart from Christ people are perishing. Reason enough for a caring evangelistic lifestyle, wouldn't you agree?

Lee Strobel, former *Chicago Tribune* reporter and atheist, says his memory of life before he was a Christian is a springboard: "Though I was undeserving, he rescued me from a life of irrelevancy and an eternity of despair." This memory moves him to let God use him "to bring people into His family."[2]

If you are someone who has been delivered from futility and rebellion, you know that God has done something great in your life. You know that what's happened to you will totally transform every life that hears and believes it. Remember the Book of Acts?

The best way to get the message of God's intervention in human destiny to the ends of the earth, and the best way to spread the word that the Messiah had come with a plan of redemption and renewal, was to send every man, woman, and child who had crossed paths with the Savior into the world. And that is precisely what happened. God salted civilization with his presence.[3]

Today, every Christian man, woman, and child delivers the same message by how they live and what they say. Lives are transformed today as they were in Acts, by such announcements.

Every day we have a pattern of activity that occurs within our circle of influence. When in that circle we point others to Jesus, we are participating in God's work of rescuing people.

Your Circle of Influence

"Lord, send some searching nonbelievers across my path this week." This is a commendable prayer because the heart longs to share Christ with those who don't know him. Is anything troublesome to you about this prayer? Perhaps not, but look more closely at the word *searching*. If you believe that God desires to use you in his ongoing work in the world and you believe that evangelism is a way of seeing and doing, primarily in your circle of influence, then you may want to let God decide who are seekers and nonseekers. I perceive an unhealthy emphasis on spending time on the people with whom we can accomplish the most. We don't always know who the true seekers are, so we must be ready to do the work of evangelism with the ones God brings our way. Many who write about evangelism emphasize what the Lord told the seventy: "one of the Lord's primary strategies: Concentrate your evangelistic efforts on those who are ready."[4] We must interact with people concerning the gospel before we know if they're ready. How quickly the emphasis changes from our being *faithful* to our being *successful*. In my life there have been few times someone said, "Randy, I am searching for him; can you help me find him?"

In his excellent book *Gentle Persuasion*, Joe Aldrich says we sow the seed with absolute confidence that God will give a harvest. Of course we must remember the timing will be his, not ours, and he also will determine the yield. We wonder why we see so few results. Those persons in whose lives God has used me only became known to me much later in my life. I remember one young man in whom I invested a great deal of time and effort. I judged his response to my work very poor. Years later I learned he became a minister and credited me as being the major influence in his life. At the time, however, he was certainly not responding enthusiastically!

In 1965 I spent the summer in Tom's River, New Jersey, knocking on doors trying to interest people in home Bible studies. I recall one lady agreeing to several Bible studies with me around her kitchen table. During each study we were constantly interrupted by her teenage son, Allen, and her daughter. The boy was a certified pest. I learned about patient endurance during the study sessions, never knowing if her tendency to become confused easily was the result of poor teaching on my part or her son's constant interruptions. Needless to say very little good was accomplished. Or so I thought. Almost ten years later I received a phone call from a friend in Oklahoma. He asked me if I knew Allen and had followed what had happened in his life. I said no. He told me he had just heard him speak in a convention on evangelism and tell the story of his conversion to Christ. He remembered my visits to his family, the Bible studies, the kindness. He says God used me to bring his mother, his sister, and him to the Lord. What an amazing story, and a humbling one, for I did not know what God was doing in those visits! We must be willing to sow with patient faith.

The Scottish writer George McDonald never knew that God awakened C. S. Lewis to faith through his writings. And Lewis didn't live to see his book used of God to turn Charles Colson to Christ. Maybe a good question is this: Are you sure you know everything God is doing? Maybe that's why "neighbor love" in the Bible is taught by principle—love your neighbor as yourself so that the only outcome we can be sure of is that it pleases God. Your neighbor's response is God's concern.

Ken Blanchard, author of *The One-Minute Manager* and other books in the management field, conducts seminars each year with managers of companies across America. Ken has been transformed by the gospel of Jesus Christ and he cares about the people he teaches. He knows they are just like him in their aspirations and disappointments. He knows that some of these people would consider the option of God in their lives, if he could visit with them one-on-one. It's a dilemma because at each seminar the time he has to interact with individuals is very limited. He attempts, whenever possible, to build a bridge of understanding between himself and the managers who come to his seminars.

Blanchard has written the story of his conversion and life lived by the power of Christ in *We Are the Beloved* (Zondervan, 1994). He writes as one who knows his readers well, and he describes how his life story was changed by the gospel story of Jesus and Jesus' love. The book is an excellent example of a man attempting to be God's instrument with his friends and associates, those with whom he has influence.

How People Become Christians

George Hunter's extensive research suggests "that the gospel spreads along the social networks of living Christians."[5] The data he and others have collected on how people become Christians makes an enormous contribution to our understanding and helps form our strategies.

Win Arn reports that in America today, between 75 and 90 percent of new church members surveyed report that a friend or relative was the factor most responsible for their coming to church. Webs of common kinship (the larger family), common friendship (friends and neighbors), and common associates (special interest groups, work relationships, and recreation associates) are still the means by which most people become Christians today.[6] Church consultant Lyle Schaller's twenty-five years of research shows that two-thirds to three-quarters of all new church members are responding to an invitation from someone in their kinship or friendship network.[7]

Reflecting on Jesus' charge in Matthew 28, to make disciples, Dennis Guernsey, then at Fuller Theological Seminary, suggested that "a disciple is one who has entered a primary relationship with God through a primary relationship with another person."

Some scholars say that one person can have meaningful relationships with as many as thirty people in a lifetime. Meaningful relationships would mean we know them well and they know us well. We have frequent, caring contact with them. We have meals together, spend leisure time together, support each other in the crises of life, and risk sharing our deepest beliefs about God, life, and spiritual reality. Jesus worked and shared his daily life with only twelve people. It was with these twelve that he had the most meaningful relationships while on earth. It's easy to see why our goals for influencing someone for Christ should start not with total strangers but with people already in our lives.

Being an Evangelistic Tool

Can you visualize living redemptively in your everyday life, seeking to do God's work in the lives of people you touch? Are you willing to see the people you come in contact with every day as "fields ripe for harvest"? If you say yes, then you can offer yourself as an evangelistic tool in God's hands by doing the following:

1. Make a list of people in your circle of influence for whom you will pray.
2. Seek to model a Christ-honoring life before them.
3. As you interact with them, attempt to understand their world—their hopes, frustrations, and fears.
4. Build friendships with them and the significant people in their lives—especially their family.
5. Watch for opportunities to serve the people and their families for whom you are praying.
6. Seize every opportunity to tell the story of what Jesus has done for you and for them.

Living consciously as God's redemptive tool forms in you a way of seeing and doing that allows God to work through you. It's not your primary task to make everybody on your list a Christian. It's your task to live in such a way that what you do and what you say may become a part of God's strategy for bringing the people on your list to himself.

5

Opportunities for Evangelism

> It is easy to have love for humanity, but it is hard to have it for one's neighbor. . . . Jesus never once told us to love humanity . . . [he] told us to love *as he did;* that is to touch and serve the specific individuals we meet.
>
> Peter Kreeft

The primary problem that limits our evangelistic outreach is not lack of motivation. We want to tell the story, but we may have been discouraged by fear of rejection. We may have been turned off by the high pressure tactics used by our peers. Or we may have been incapacitated by guilt about what we didn't do in the past. Bill Hybels says, "Authentic evangelism is never motivated by guilt."[1]

Evangelism will not happen unless our primary motivation is love for people. I want to encourage you to develop a heart for people—a mind-set that serves with a redemptive goal—that allows you to be God's instrument in people's lives. When we learn from Jesus' lifestyle to "major" in people, God uses us to bring them to him. You don't have to become someone you are not to influence people toward God. Each person's unique personality and evangelistic style imprints the lives of those around him or her.

Evangelism Styles

Let's look for a moment at the different evangelistic styles available for our use. This is just a sample of the possible styles, for as we evaluate the need and adjust our style accordingly, styles of evangelism become unlimited in number. You may find that you have already developed a style that is similar to ones represented here.

First, consider Peter's style in Acts 2. He was *confrontational:* "This Jesus, whom you crucified" (v. 36). Some call Peter's sermon "announcement evangelism." Some radio preachers use this direct style and it is often effective because the one using it is not deterred by circumstances or by who may be listening. It may be unsuccessful at times, however, because it may fail to take into account where people are in their lives in terms of their openness to the truth. Some people may consider the boldness to be insensitivity.

Paul in his Mars Hill speech to the Athenians used an appeal to their intellect with careful reasoning, and one result was that "some of the Jews were persuaded" (Acts 17:4). This could be called an *evidential* approach to evangelism. Today, speakers like Ravi Zacharias and Alistair

McGrath use reasoning and evidence as they present the Christian message. This approach will be effective with those who have erected intellectual barriers to belief. The person who wants to evangelize with this approach must know his audience well.

As I speak on *A Caring Touch,* a daily radio program designed to reach hurting, searching people, I try to use a compassionate approach that suggests to listeners that Jesus offers real hope for their lives. This might be called a *prescriptive* style of evangelism. Charles Stanley uses this style on his program *In Touch* in Atlanta. This style is effective when it speaks to the particular need of the listener. Those who are not feeling an urgent need may not be moved by the message.

Another style especially popular in America today is the *testimonial* approach. "Once I was lost but now I'm found." The emphasis is on the contrast between the before-Christ life and the radical transformation Christ has brought about. The testimonies of well-known personalities who have become Christians are examples of this approach to evangelism. It will be effective with people who feel that their lives are at a dead end, people who are searching for an answer. The testimonial approach can be very effective with friends and relatives, as they not only hear about the changes Christ has made, but see them lived out. Many people "just need a solid, sane, normal Christian to share with them a slice of their transformed life."[2]

There is also a *relational* style of evangelism. Joe Aldrich of Multnomah College calls it "friendship evangelism." It's the approach that is seen in the way we serve and meet the needs of others. Dorcas in Acts 9 illustrates the lifestyle that serves people's needs, helps meet crises, gives a cup of cold water because of Jesus, and so points people to God. This approach is very effective with the limited number of people with whom we can interact at this level each day. It requires a deep and long-term commitment and a humble attitude on our part.

Another style that many use is the *invitational* style. This is the approach we use when we invite people to attend our church or come to a Bible study, a concert, or other event. This may be the approach of choice for people who are introverted and feel more comfortable inviting people to "come and see" rather than confronting or sharing directly.

This tends to be a hit-or-miss approach. It depends on the experience of the person attending the church service or concert whether or not it has an impact. As I've noted elsewhere in this book, a personal approach is often the most effective.

I'm reminded of a conversation I had with Dr. Jack Reese, who has given careful study to how people become converted to Christ. He notes that very few people are converted all of a sudden through one experience. Usually conversion results from a series of events and interactions. A worthwhile goal for us is to seek to be one link in the chain of someone's conversion. What role we play is not significant; that we are willing to play the role we can is all-important.

Avenues for the Gospel

Neighbor Love

William Dyrness, professor of theology and culture at Fuller Seminary in Pasadena, California, has made a careful study, *How Does America Hear the Gospel?* which is extremely helpful for understanding what people around us value and how the gospel can be spoken in ways they can hear. He observes, "Our failing marriages, our profound loneliness, and our desperate search for ourselves" make us unusually open to "expressions of the gospel [that] deal with issues of relationship and personal identity." He believes "the major single problem for American social life is the problem of relationships—we do not understand them and cannot maintain them."[3]

The strong emphasis in our society on individualism and self-reliance doesn't serve us well. We're estranged from God and from each other. So the gospel of reconciliation is desperately needed. Some will determine it worthy of consideration, especially if people's lives demonstrate its effectiveness. Dyrness says we can reach out to Americans in several ways.

First, we must share the stresses and hopes of others. So many suffer from some difficult emotional pain and our evangelism will not be effective if we don't share the pressures and joys of individuals and of our community. We should acknowledge the problems with relationships and tell the truth about life's hurts. Then we can stress that God loves each person.

Americans are looking for signs of transcendence, Dyrness says. Is there a larger story than our pressures and joys? When a child dies or a job is lost, ultimate questions arise: Does someone outside us care? Is there someone to lean on? Christians need to answer these questions for their neighbors. We must make it clear that God knows and cares about each individual's pain.

In our presentation of the challenge of the gospel, then, Dyrness says we need to make clear that our hopes and disappointments take on different meaning in light of what God has done for us in Jesus Christ. We need to show our neighbors that in the cross, God was in Christ—taking our suffering and giving birth to our hope for a better future. God is our best, and in one sense only, friend. He has solved the problem that kept us separated from each other and from him.

Finally, says Dyrness, there's the issue of obedience. Those being challenged by the gospel must respond by taking action. They must become involved with what God has done and is doing. As people become Christ's disciples, the gospel works reconciliation in their lives. Then as Christians they go to suffering people and serve them. The cycle of evangelism continues.[4]

James Packer explains that "neighbor love" is the reason we concern ourselves with understanding people's felt needs: "My neighbor's deepest need is to know the love of God in Jesus Christ, and my claim to love him or her is hollow if I make no attempt to meet that need as best I can."[5]

The popular writer Peter Kreeft points out:

It is easy to have love for humanity, but it is hard to have it for one's neighbor. Humanity never surprises you, never disappoints you, never bugs you. Jesus never once told us to love humanity . . . [he] told us to love *as he did;* that is to touch and serve the specific individuals we meet.[6]

Steve Sjogren teaches the values of servant evangelism. In *Conspiracy of Kindness* he asks, "In what specific ways do those who live in your city need help, healing and wholeness? What could we do to touch these people with God's kingdom in a practical way?"[7] Christians who do deeds of service in their city say their goal is "to show God's love in a practical way."

By meeting people's felt needs, Sjogren believes Christians are participating in the process of evangelism, and God provides opportunities to explain the gospel message. He's convinced that "every person is at a unique place in their gradual awakening to the love of Christ." The Christian may be making initial contact with a person or watering seeds sown by others. What happens next isn't created by external pressures or unrealistic expectations. "I planted the seed, Apollos watered it, but God made it grow. So neither he who plants nor he who waters is anything, but only God, who makes things grow" (1 Cor. 3:6–7).

In a hurry up, impersonal world this personal, caring contact sometimes makes people open to other Christian relationships. This should not become an approach primarily with strangers but a way of serving those in our circles of influence. Sjogren says he's made five discoveries through his effort:

1. People listen when I treat them like friends.
2. When I serve, hearts are touched.
3. As I serve, I redefine the perception of a Christian.
4. Doing the message precedes telling the message.
5. Focus on planting, not harvesting.[8]

Camilla and I have seventeen years of experience in meeting the felt needs that develop in people's lives during times of chronic and life-threatening illness and times of grief. By serving people in these times, occasions develop for telling the story. Not always, of course, but sometimes, and sometimes in surprising ways.

Small Group Support

One of the highlights of studying at Fuller Seminary was eating a Japanese sushi dinner with Dr. Dennis Guernsey. He knew my interest in encouraging Christians to use their everyday lives as opportunities to influence people for Christ. Little did I realize, as I looked forward to dinner with Dr. Guernsey, that I was about to experience two surprises. The first was the sushi, which he wanted me to enjoy as much as he did. The second—more appealing—was his enthusiastic report of what churches in Korea are doing to reach the lost through the lives of everyday Christians.

Dennis took a large napkin, spread it on the table, and diagrammed the strategy that twelve congregations (with average memberships of six hundred) used over a five- to seven-year period. God blessed them with growth of between three thousand and five thousand members. The strategy involved meeting on Sunday for worship, the Lord's Supper, and encouragement. Then on Tuesdays, Thursdays, and Saturdays small groups of members met in someone's home in their part of the city. The purpose of the home meetings was to study the Bible, discuss their network of family and friends, pray for them, and devise ways to serve them in times of family crisis.

The small group of Christians served whatever need arose with skill and sensitivity, willing to speak about God's provisions but under no compulsion. Studies for the Christian small groups centered on how Jesus treated people and the crises people experience over the course of the life cycle.

The Korean believers intentionally structured their strategy with the goal of outreach with the gospel to their network of family and friends. Prayer and compassionate Christian service led them to people who were moved by God's Spirit to come to Christ. This approach creates in Christians a mind-set for evangelism in the course of their everyday life's activities.

A home group might have a grandmother rearing two school-age grandchildren alone, a married couple with an eleven-year-old daughter, two older couples with four grown children, and three single professionals—a total of seventeen. Each one would make a list of perhaps six people—family members, work associates, neighbors—that he or she wants to see come to the Lord. The group then agrees to pray for, learn about, and serve these people for the glory of God: a total of 102 people become the focus of loving concern. In Korea new Christians are born from these lists.

In our own country small group evangelism has been used effectively for years by groups like InterVarsity Christian Fellowship's evangelistic Bible studies and Campus Crusade for Christ's action groups. Richard Peace, professor of evangelism at Fuller, wrote an excellent paperback training guide, *Small Group Evangelism: A Training Program for Reaching Out with the Gospel.* It's based on the premise that a few will come to our churches, but many will come into our homes.[9] This small book shows how groups in homes provide a non-threatening atmosphere where believers and those not yet committed openly explore the Christian faith and the person of Jesus together. It also provides a nine-week program for training in small group evangelism.

Crisis and Caring

Dr. Frank Pittman, a psychiatrist, is the past president of the American Association of Marriage and Family Therapists. He describes a crisis as "a state of things in which a decisive change one way or the other is impending."[10]

It's possible to have a crisis that does not result in change, but the opportunity for a new perspective on values is substantial. People are open to changes in worldview, value system, and commitments during times of disequilibrium in their lives. When they face transitions or crises without adequate resources for understanding and adjusting to them, they often come to the end of themselves and become open to new possibilities.

There are four categories of crises:

Bolts from the blue—sudden death, house burning down, child injured seriously.

Developmental crises—marriage; birth of children; children starting school, going through puberty, becoming independent and leaving home; parents growing older, retiring, aging, and dying. There can be crises of teen promiscuity and pregnancy, drug use, school problems, marital infidelity, mid-life, divorce.

Structural crises—families with an alcoholic member, violent or adulterous members; multiple job losses.

Caretaker crises—welfare families, chronic mental or physical illness (one or more members are non-functional and dependent).

Some of the family stress literature suggests the average American family experiences moderate to severe crises once every four years. The crisis may be moderate, such as a car accident resulting in a serious leg injury, or the first child becoming a driving teenager. Then the crisis may be the father's diagnosis of lung cancer or parents' deciding to divorce. Following the onset of crises a period of opportunity often follows. The family system is most vulnerable to change during the next six weeks. In this period family members may express feelings of powerlessness ("out of control"), meaninglessness ("This makes no sense"), isolation ("I just don't know how to cope"), or self-estrangement ("If only I had . . ." or "I'm beat up inside").

As we see the need to minister to people in crisis we will please God by meeting real human need. In a receptive climate a relationship may be formed that will lead to opportunities to share Christ and his cross. Christians will want to learn the dynamics involved in people's crises. From time to time churches have asked me how to connect with people in these times. Among my suggestions, I propose a series of quarterly events that relate to the transition times in the life cycle. Since transition times that are met with inadequate resources bring times of crisis for people, the church is wise to "put a face on Christ" to the community, showing love, understanding, and solidarity and sharing the struggle with people as we search for solutions with them.

What follows is a two-year program that an Oklahoma church designed to address their community's concerns:

Year 1

Spring Event: "Making Good Marriages Better"
Spring Event: "Aging Parents—The Brighter Alternatives"
Early Fall Event: "Parenting Is Not for Cowards," "Teaching Values to Your Child," "How To Really Love Your Teenager"
Later Fall Event: "Helping a Loved One through Grief—Preparing for the Holidays"

Year 2

Spring Event: "Divorce Recovery—Rebuilding Your Life"
Spring Event: "Are You Fit to Be Tied? Preparing for Marriage"
Fall Event: "Parenting Grown Children," "Loving the Empty Nest"

Fall Event: "Beginning Your Family Right," "Affair-Proof Your Marriage"

Notice this program creates a mentality for family outreach and is not heavily crisis centered. Bruce Powers in *Growing Faith: How It Develops and How It Can Be Nurtured* discusses developmental conversion, crisis conversion, and process conversion. Developmental conversion focuses on a progressive pattern of faith development that parallels developmental phases. Crisis conversion is rooted in the tension of unusual or painful circumstances, and relief comes with a major reorientation in beliefs and lifestyle. Process conversion takes place over a long period of time as maturity in the gospel takes place. People are at different places in life and respond according to how they hear that Jesus makes a difference in their lives.[11]

If families have a moderate to severe crisis every three to four years, then probably one-third to one-quarter of our families in a local church are in some crisis at any given time. Will we be there for each other? When people deal with real-life issues in a supportive, affirming, and hope-filled faith community, they can experience God's healing and empowering love. My experience tells me that a fellowship that isn't able to give this kind of support will not have the tools necessary to minister to outsiders in crisis. What I'm talking about starts in the family, where love and support is given unconditionally. It is then practiced in the church family, and finally can be offered to those who have yet to experience the love of God that brings restoration, reconciliation, renewal, and power to cope with life's challenges.

A word of caution is needed here. When you want to help people in crisis there are two dangers: First, that you'll step in and try to fix things for them, taking charge of their lives; and second, that you'll prematurely be verbally direct about Jesus being the solution to whatever the problem is. This can be a turnoff to those who don't know Christ as Savior. We may fall into either of these dangers because we become uncomfortable with people's problems, and to meet our needs we quickly offer solutions that may, in fact, interfere with God's working in their lives. The caring Christian learns to live with the tension and pain in others' lives. As Henri Nouwen said, "Care is the basis for cure." Remember, your goal is to please God by serving people. Listening well is supremely important. A crisis may lead a person to deal with the deep questions, and God may use you at the right time to speak about the good news of Christ. Avoid becoming what William McKay calls the "crisis vulture," and never take advantage of people being down—even when you think it's for their own good."[12]

I like what David Bosch, author of *Transforming Mission,* says about serving people who are experiencing life's crises:

> To those who are experiencing personal tragedy, emptiness, loneliness, estrangement, and meaninglessness the gospel does come as peace, comfort, fullness and joy. But the gospel offers this only within the context of it being a word about the lordship of Christ in all realms of life.[13]

So while we need to be sensitive in our timing, when we serve others in Jesus' name we desire to eventually give them the whole story of God's love in Christ.

6

Special Arenas
for Evangelism

The question that truly counts is not whether we
imitate Mother Teresa, but whether we are open to
the many little sufferings of those with whom we
share our life. True compassion always begins where
we are.

Henri Nouwen

It would be easy to conclude that ministering "where
you are" in the normal flow of your life is all you should
do. But if you are an upper-middle-class Christian and you
focus on your neighborhood, family, friends, and work
place, you may never come into contact with anyone who
is poor, racially different from you, educationally superior

to you, or financially wealthy. These people are also a part of your world. You may need to take action to involve yourself with them. Why should you do this? Because God has blessings for you in your interaction with those different from you.

While I was living in Nashville, I often drove to the heart of the city to work with inner city youth and their families. I shudder to think what I would have missed had I passed by the opportunity to know those young people. The facility called Youth Hobby Shop offered me the blessing of caring for those whose lives were marked by family breakup, violence, insecurity, and fear. Yet many of those I met knew and trusted God more completely than I did. They taught me how to grow in faith, hope, and love. My involvement occurred during the time of racial unrest in the '60s. Tension between Blacks and Whites was real. It was during this period that I began to learn to reject stereotypes. The poor may be rich; the rich often are poor.

The Gospel for the Rich

I'm amazed that so many Christians resent the rich. We lack interest in the real-life concerns of these people, I suppose, because we assume that they couldn't possibly have any. Do we overlook the part of the story of the rich young ruler where Scripture says, "Jesus looked upon him and loved him"? Maybe Jesus—but not us. Don't gauge spiritual hunger to be absent from an affluent person.[1] We must avoid feelings of jealousy for we can easily resent the power affluent people seem to exercise in our everyday lives.

If we make an effort to develop friendships with those we consider rich, we may be surprised at how receptive to genuine friendship they are. The appearance of self-sufficiency may mask problems of life for which they would welcome spiritual solutions.

The Gospel for the Poor

Jesus displaced himself when he left glory for a barn. That barn was a lot farther from where we live than we may want to admit. We can't read Scripture without seeing the special concern God has for the poor. We who love God should have great interest for the special concerns of our Father. The gospel must be shared with the poor for us to be able to understand it better and possess it more deeply ourselves. I've seen my need for God best when I've spent time loving the poor. They show me God in ways I never see him unless I'm with them. I don't find it mysterious at all to read the spiritually mature writing of the Nun of Calcutta, Mother Teresa. She's been taught by the poor.

Jesus told us, "Whatever you did for one of the least of these . . . you did for me" (Matt. 25:40). For some strange reason many of us who want to do something for Jesus won't do anything for "the least of these"—the poor. Devotional writings help us with the spiritual life, as do worship and spiritual friendship, but we also will see his face in the faces of the poor. If we go to them they will teach us. Many Christians pass over opportunities to share the gospel with the poor.

My friend Dr. Harold Shank works among the poor in Memphis. The work is difficult, and he speaks very little about its successes. With great resolution he keeps on going, for he knows that's where he's supposed to be. God is doing his work *among* the poor—and *through* them.

Family Evangelism

Reader's Digest (July 1991) featured an article called "The Kids of Kent Amos." Kent Amos is fifty-one. He moved back to his home town of Washington, D.C., about thirteen years ago. From an entry level position as a sales trainee at Xerox he rose to be director of the corporate staff. He had a wife, Carmen, and two stepchildren—Wesley, sixteen, and Debbie, ten.

His biggest concern in selecting housing was where would be a place for good schooling for his children. He didn't really want to take them to the section of Washington where he had grown up, because that section had declined into a crime-ridden, inner-city neighborhood, complete with low-income families and troubled teenagers. Why put Wesley and Debbie at risk when he could afford a better place to live and a better school for his children to attend? Yet he moved back to his old neighborhood. His heart sank when his boy began to bring home friends from his basketball team at school. He said to himself, *They're thugs,* and worried about what was going to happen to his children.

It had been ten years since he had been in Vietnam as an army lieutenant. He'd had command over some difficult situations. But what could he do to help his children in inner-city Washington? He made a decision to help his children reach out to the children around them by making his home a safe place for kids.

Kent was determined to help change his kids' friends. He said to these children, "You are welcome in this house. Here you will be treated like our own kids. But we'll also hold you to the standards that we set for them."

The youths learned, for example, that when they took their jackets off they were not just to throw them on the furniture, they were to hang them up. If they reached a door before Carmen got there, they were to open it for her. Before dinner they were to pause, because a prayer of grace would be said. They were to keep their elbows off the table. They also were encouraged to talk about themselves.

Kent noticed that the word *father* almost never came up. One boy named T-bone wouldn't mention his father, because both his father and his stepfather were in prison. "Always remember," Kent told this boy, "our home is your home."

Milton, a seventeen-year-old sophomore who liked to play basketball, lived with a working aunt and spent most of his free time at home alone, a latchkey kid. He'd flunked the eighth grade, which left him a year behind. Kent said to him, "You've got to get your priorities straight, son. The reason for school is education. Basketball comes second."

Milton had no memories of his own father but he figured out that Kent must be like a father because he laid down the law. He cared enough to tell him there were standards. So Milton began staying with the Amoses at night. He enjoyed dinner. He enjoyed the conversation, and he listened carefully as Kent talked about Black opportunities and achievement. When Milton left, it was always with a hug from the man of the house.

One day, after Milton had spent a particularly long period of time out on the street, he came to the house and talked about some of his schoolwork problems. Kent sat down and worked with him, and there was some improvement. He said to the boy, "Do well in school tomorrow, and when you come home we'll take in a movie together." When they came home from the movie, Kent said as he sent the boy off, "See you later"—and the boy said, "Thanks, Dad."

Andre, eighteen, had a drug problem. Kent would help him. Then Andre would fall back into drugs. Kent challenged him and affirmed him. Andre would fall again. But Kent said to Andre, "We're playing at real lives here, and we'll never stop trying with you."

April Dawson lived in the inner city of Detroit but read about Kent. As she read she wondered if that kind of person really existed. She had once dreamed of excelling at school, going off to college, and escaping the inner city of Detroit. But the academic talent that had won her admission to a good high school had been soured because of some hard living that she'd done.

After she failed two classes, she struggled to make them up in summer school and worked nights at a candy store. April would sit on her bed at night and stare at the magazine photograph she had clipped of Kent Amos surrounded by some teenagers. They looked so happy. She wrote him a letter and told him how much she admired him. She said, "Those kids are lucky to have a father like you. I wish I had one. Washington, D.C., is a world away from Detroit."

Then one August evening the phone rang. "Hello April," said the quiet voice at the other end of the line. "This is your father."

"My father!?"

"How many people have you asked to be your father in the last few months?" the man coaxed.

"Mr. Amos!"

Kent Amos uses his home and family life as a natural means to allow God's love to flow through him to the lives of others. All Christians can make a commitment to use their family relationships as opportunities to serve the real needs of people.

Walter Brueggemann in *Biblical Perspectives on Evangelism* says,

> The present crisis of evangelism is in a great measure because the community of the church has not persuaded our own young of the power or validity of the gospel. I suspect that has happened because adults have been inarticulate with the family of faith about our faith.[2]

I want to ask you, Is your family an inclusive, redemptive family?

A few years ago, Tim came to live with our family. At the time we had a twenty-one-year-old daughter, who was a senior in college; a nineteen-year-old son, a senior in high school; a seventeen-year-old daughter, who was a junior in high school; and a thirteen-year-old daughter in middle school. Tim was a senior in high school, and his family lived in the inner city. They had struggles. We invited Tim to live with us because he was a good friend to our son, Mark. We thought that Tim could encourage Mark to finish high school, and we thought Mark could encourage Tim in his life. God taught us a lot through Tim. As we loved him, he grew; as we loved him, *we* grew. Our children caught a tremendous spirit of broadening family through service. And Tim and Mark helped each other finish school.

Late one Friday night, after Tim and Mark had come in, Tim sat down beside me in the den and said, "Mr. Becton, I just want you to know that I think your family's great and I really appreciate your letting me be a part of it." The doubts I had when Tim came flashed across my mind. But the true feeling in my heart flowed out as I let him know how thankful we were that he was a part of our family.

We are to be a redemptive people because we have been redeemed. We offer hope because we remember having no hope. We're inclusive rather than exclusive because we were no people, and God made us his people by his grace. God is our father, Jesus is our brother, and deliverance is our theme song. This deliverance drives us to reach out to each other, starting with each member of our family, giving restoration, reconciliation, peace, and hope. It drives us to set places at our family table for people who are not in our immediate family. We welcome people into our family and hope one day to welcome them into the larger family of God.

Paul called the Ephesian believers the household of God. It's a redemptive community. But that redemption is going to have to be practiced in our homes, because that's where God intended for the faith to be passed along.

We are a society that cocoons in our own homes. We don't want anybody to come in because we're tired of this world and its screaming demands. That is Satan's strategy to get us to close our doors. We must resist and be redemptive to families, because it's in our homes that we give the love that empowers people to become healthy and whole.

In *The Cruciform Church* Leonard Allen points out that the cross should be at the center of our conversations, because it's the center of our hope. The cross allows us to have access to God. We need cross-centered families.[3] What would they look like? Their table-talk would be uplifting and hopeful, yet realistic, facing real struggles with honesty and vulnerability. They would talk about God as the reason they have life and hope and a future.

A cross-centered family forgives each other. They don't hold grudges. Parents forgive children. Parents ask children to forgive them. Forgiveness is that marvelous lubricant that makes family relationships work, and the cross allows them to apply it liberally. Cross-centered families bind up wounds. They pour out their hearts for other people like Kent Amos does. They welcome others into their home. "There are chairs at our table for our own children and for their friends." This is evangelism. The lonely, the neglected, the abused—those like Kent Amos invited—we can invite to our table.

Cross-centered families have agape love for each other and for those they invite in. They forget about self and put the needs of others first.

Before you invite people to worship assemblies, before you invite them to special events and programs, invite them to your table in your home. Nourish them there, heal their hurts there, affirm their dreams there. They will see evidence of the impact of the gospel on your family and perhaps witness some of your joy in the Lord. Their best path to God's table may go through your house. You may have the opportunity to talk openly with them about the difference Christ makes in your family life.

Oikos is the Greek word for household. In Acts 16 the jailor and his household—*oikos*—came to Christ. Joe Aldrich encourages Christians to develop an "oikos perspective" so they can visualize the gospel flowing down webs of relationships, reaching individual after individual who know and are somehow related to each other.[4]

At some point you may feel the time is right to begin a home Bible study with the people you have invited in. There are many resources available, including study guides and videos, to help you reach non-Christians with the gospel. There are two guides that I recommend: *Your Home a Lighthouse: Hosting an Evangelistic Bible Study,* by Bob and Betty Jacks, a step-by-step manual that tells you how to get started; and *Introducing Jesus: Starting an Investigative Bible Study for Seekers,* by Peter Scazzero, a six-week study.

While traveling in the Ukraine and Russia during the collapse of communism in 1991, I visited with Christians who wanted to be instruments of God in winning their family members and friends to the Lord. Fellow evangelist Glenn Owen and I spoke to standing-room-only crowds at the Motorcyclist Hall in Kiev. On several occasions we would visit with people who had great interest in the Christian faith. Often they would stop talking until their spouse or family members could join us. They wanted their loved ones to hear the good news of God's love that they were hearing. How right they were!

Believers in Business

Through the kindness of the H. E. Butt Foundation I wrote much of this book at Wayfarer's Cottage, a house out in the woods near Leakey, Texas. As I was leaving once to return to work, I stopped at the administrative offices in Kerrville to visit with the executive director, Dr. Howard Hovde, a special friend. In discussing this book, he asked if I'd seen the new book, *Believers in Business,* written by a former professor at the Harvard Business School, Dr. Laura Nash. Dr. Nash, Howard told me, had spoken with more than eighty-five Christian CEOs across America and asked them how they lived the Christian faith in the world of commerce.[5]

The research included how these Christian business-people spoke about their faith and demonstrated their faith among the people who worked for them. These nonspecial-ists, these everyday Christians, want desperately to influ-ence people for God. What do they do, how and when do they do it, and what happens as a result? These leaders want those who work with them to know the first priority in their life is the Christian faith, but they seek to communicate in ways that do not invade the privacy or exploit a power advantage over people. Some try to "keep their witnessing low-key by creating passive opportunities to express their faith."[6]

One CEO offers to pray for employees when he learns of some distress in their life. Another held a formal dedi-cation of his office to the service of God and invited his employees. Those interviewed utilize special opportunities because they believe the story of what God did in Christ needs to come to businesspeople "from somebody who shares their world."[7] They know people are watching to see if they are living a Christ-centered existence.

CEO Fred Smith cautions that leaders should be quick to live the faith and slow to speak it in the business setting. The former provides the opportunity for the latter away from the office.

Since I was a child I've known of the commitment of the Ezell family to live the Christian faith in their busi-ness, Purity Dairies, in Nashville, Tennessee. I know em-ployees who opened their lives to God because of their example.

Christians are influencing others in business every day. God is at work. Those Christians live and speak about their faith in Christ where possible and appropriate. They have little concern for the possibility of scorn and ridicule.

Some attend group Bible studies or prayer groups with other businesspeople for strength and encouragement. Their goal is to be faithful to the one who has called them to himself and to the world in redemptive service. This needs to be our goal too, in whatever arena God has placed us for evangelism.

7

The Role
of Your Church

While serving as director of family outreach for the
Herald of Truth during the eighties, I often read about Baby
Boomers—that group of Americans born between 1946
and 1964. The year was 1989 when I read that more than
one million Baby Boomers had joined churches, coming
back to the organized religion that they had rejected as teens
and college students. In their late twenties and early thir-

ties they married and bore children. As they reared their children they became interested in teaching them morals and values, deciding perhaps churches could help.

What kind of churches have the Baby Boomers found appealing? Churches that are happy, at peace, and biblically conservative and that provide meaningful programs for training children.

Data on Baby Boomers helped provide the foundation for a new emphasis in many congregations: the seeker-sensitive worship service, pioneered by churches like Willow Creek in Illinois, Saddleback in California, and hundreds of others. The goal of these churches is to provide an atmosphere where non-Christians will feel comfortable so that they'll come, hear the gospel, and accept Christ as Savior.

What about the congregation where you are a member? How would visitors describe your church service? Friendly? biblical? helpful and relevant to everyday life?

Ed Dobson wrote *Starting a Seeker-Sensitive Service: How Traditional Churches Can Reach the Unchurched,* the story of a church in Grand Rapids, Michigan, that has taken serious steps to reach unchurched people. Ed Dobson says:

> The work grew out of five years of ministry to hurting people who are either skeptics, agnostics, or doubters of the Christian faith. It has been shaped by people who do not give much of a rip about God or the Bible, but they are at least willing to listen.[1]

I know what happens at church makes a difference to people. It can either encourage people to come or turn them away. What concerns me most is, Will they hear the story at church? Alan Sell reminds us that "no Christian can remove the offense of the Cross. It is scandalous in the *sense* of being a stumbling block. The Christian faith [says] at the Cross-Resurrection God acted once and for all for the salvation of the world."[2]

Faith and Deeds

Hearing the story isn't enough, however; I want anyone who comes to church to hear the gospel *and* see it in the lives of those in whom it has taken hold. Gareth Icenogle observes:

Groups who know how to help members find meaning and healing through pain become good evangelists in a world full of pain. The world is hungry to find a community of caring persons who can pronounce the forgiveness and healing of Christ to their pain. The group who carries such wounded persons to Christ and sees them made whole becomes an attractive family to the outside world.[3]

Again, "if the church is to impart to the world a message of hope and love, of faith, justice and peace, something of this should become visible, audible, and tangible in the church itself." People are watching, and they should be. They won't see perfection, but they should see "a radiant manifestation of the Christian faith."[4]

The New Testament envisions a Christian lifestyle of loving hospitality that will accompany the verbal invitation to join God's own fellowship. When people see our lives, they should see the values of the kingdom of God. Then we're really saying to them, "You see, this is what I mean by the gospel."[5]

Evangelism and Worship

I spoke for a great church in Savannah, Tennessee, on a Sunday when the emphasis for the morning was explaining the faith to those there who normally did not attend. Families brought neighbors, and a number left that day understanding the story of redemption perhaps for the first time. This can be done three or four times a year with good results.

I believe warmth and kindness is an essential church atmosphere every Sunday. But what happens in the service should center on believers. Just as in the home, visitors are welcome to overhear the gospel. My concern in the public worship of the church is more about the *content* of the gospel and *comportment* of the worshipers than the *commendation* of the visitor—as much as I hope he or she is moved toward God.

Jack Hayford is the senior minister of The Church On The Way in Van Nuys, California. Last fall his congregation was receiving an average of fifty new members through conversion every month. He believes the amazing growth of his church came about "because God taught us a path of evangelism through our commitment to worship."[6] Jack believes in overt evangelism but he also believes that when God's people focus on praise and worship they can't help becoming "God's magnet, drawing people from darkness into light."

I interviewed two visitors to the church, and both told me of the amazing attractiveness of church people who are grateful for what God has done and is doing in their lives. Jack Hayford believes God's people worship because of who he is and his worthiness to be worshiped. That this worship opens the outsider to consider the gospel for his life is a by-product. It's when God's people scatter from their corporate worship into the world that evangelism takes place. We go as "agents of reconciliation, compassion, and peace."[7] I agree with my friend Dr. André Resner, who suggests that worship services could well begin "with a call for all present who have not been baptized into Christ to receive [Christian baptism] after which the call to worship would then begin."[8] Worship of God is for those who have accepted God's gift and desire his rule in their lives. God invites every outsider to become an insider.

It was my privilege to study evangelism in the fall of 1994 with Dr. George Hunter, dean of the Asbury Theological Seminary's School of World Mission and Evangelism. He related story after story of churches that were doing effective evangelism using the church building not only for Sunday worship but also for events through the week.

I am eager to say Christians should invite their family, friends, and associates to meaningful events where the gospel is shared, but my hope is that we will not depend on the Sunday morning service to do our evangelizing for us. God desires us to live an evangelistic lifestyle every day so that the gospel is out among the people where they live. Church building evangelism is mostly a modern phenomenon; the New Testament church shared the good news wherever they were. It seems as though it was impossible for them not to. F. F. Bruce called the movement of the Christian message through first century society "a spreading flame."

A Balance

Of course, we need both lifestyle and church evangelism. The temptation may be, however, just to "let the church do it"; that's why I am emphasizing everyday evangelism.

Nevertheless, our churches certainly are also part of God's evangelistic work. The beautiful work *I Stand by the Door* by Samuel Shoemaker describes the attitude churches and church members need to have toward unbelievers. His writing emphasizes God's eagerness to have people in church and the timidity and fears many people feel because the church fails to welcome them.

> I stand by the door. I neither go too far in, nor stay too far out. The door is the most important door in the world—it is the door through which men walk when they find God. There's no use my going way inside, and staying there, when so many are still outside and they, as much as I, crave to know where the door is. And all that so many ever find is only the wall where a door ought to be. They creep along the wall like blind men, with outstretched, groping hands. Feeling for a door, knowing there must be a door, yet they never find it . . . So I stand by the door.
>
> The most tremendous thing in the world is for people to find that door—the door to God. The most important thing anyone can do is to take hold of one of those blind, groping hands, and put it on the latch—the latch that only clicks and opens to the man's own touch. Men die outside the door, as starving beggars die on cold nights in cruel cities in the dead of winter—die for want of what is within their grasp. They live, on the other side of it—live because they have not found it. Nothing else matters compared with helping them find it, and open it, and walk in, and find Him . . . So I stand at the door.
>
> Go in, great saints, go all the way in—go way down into the cavernous cellars, and way up into the spacious attics. It is a vast, roomy house, this house where God is. Go

into the deepest of hidden casements, of withdrawal, of silence, of sainthood. Some must inhabit those inner rooms, and know the depths and heights of God, and call outside to the rest of us how wonderful it is. Sometimes I take a deeper look in, sometimes venture in a little farther; but my place seems closer to the opening . . . So I stand by the door.

There is another reason why I stand there. Some people get part way in and become afraid lest God and the zeal of His house devour them; for God is so very great, and asks all of us. And these people feel a cosmic claustrophobia, and want to get out. "Let me out!" they cry. And the people way inside only terrify them more. Somebody must be by the door to tell them that they are spoiled for the old life, they have seen too much: once taste God, and nothing but God will do any more. Somebody must be watching for the frightened who seek to sneak out just where they came in, to tell them how much better it is inside. The people too far in do not see how near these are to leaving—preoccupied with the wonder of it all. Somebody must watch for those who have entered the door, but some would like to run away. So for them, too, I stand by the door. I admire the people who go way in. But I wish they would not forget how it was before they got in. Then they would be able to help the people who have not yet even found the door, or the people who want to run away again from God.

You can go in too deeply, and stay in too long, and forget the people outside the door. As for me, I shall take my accustomed place, near enough to God to hear him, and know he is there, but not so far from men as not to hear them, and remember they are there, too. Where? Outside the door—thousands of them, millions of them.

But—more important for me—one of them, two of them, ten of them, whose hands I am intended to put on the latch. So I shall stand by the door and wait for those who seek it. "I had rather be a door-keeper . . ." So I stand by the door.

8

Training for Telling Your Story

Christianity is not a statistical view of life. That there should be more joy in heaven over one sinner who repents than over all the hosts of the just, is an anti-statistical proposition.

Malcolm Muggeridge

Do you remember the day you said yes to God—the day you became a Christian? You responded to this announcement: "The time has come at last—the kingdom of God has arrived. You must change your hearts and minds and believe the good news" (Mark 1:15 PHILLIPS).

At that moment God came to you in Jesus Christ and met you in your deepest need, reconciling you to himself. Forgiveness and salvation were given to you. This message changed you and will still change the world. That's why God calls you to bear witness to Jesus Christ in everything you do, so that all may know the truth of what God has done.

While you and I are familiar with the ideas and images of salvation, we need to review them frequently in order to be effective witnesses. This review helps us remember that "God has a vision for the salvation, the making whole, of society as well."[1]

Paul says Christ died for our sins, bringing forgiveness to us, making us whole, restoring us to fellowship with God. God was reconciling the world to himself in Christ, and we now have the message and ministry of reconciliation in the world (2 Cor. 5:18–21). We've been justified. This is all God's doing and is his gift to those who place their trust in Christ.

John Newton summarized his conversion to Christ this way: "Amazing grace! how sweet the sound that saved a wretch like me! I once was lost but now am found, was blind but now I see."

Your story of deliverance should find a place in your conversations. Psalm 107:2 says what is expected of grateful people: "Let the redeemed of the LORD say so."

We will be encouraged in our effort to tell the story if we meet occasionally with a small group of Christians for fellowship, rehearsal of our story, and discussions of our opportunities for service and witness in our everyday lives. Our strategic plan can be solidified with a list of people for whom we and our friends are praying.

My Story

Here is my story as an example.

My life was given to me because of the grace and kindness of God, who is the giver of everything and the one to thank for every gift.

I was born in Nashville, Tennessee, September 17, 1944, the second of four children given to Harold and Myrna Becton. Dad worked on the railroad and held a second full-time job as a master carpenter. Mother was highly intelligent and gifted as an artist and writer.

Life was hard for my family because my father drank heavily. Family life was often chaotic and upsetting. Twice Mother had nervous breakdowns. However, with the loving care of God and the help of Christian friends my childhood and teenage years were marked by positive experiences.

Because I grew to be six feet, six and one-half inches tall, and loved sports, I excelled in basketball and baseball, winning a basketball scholarship to David Lipscomb University, a Christian college in Nashville. I also wrestled during my college years and wanted to be a coach, counselor, or minister. Some say I eventually became all three, but *minister* means the most to me.

In my third year of college I was wrestling with life's purpose and meaning, especially with whether God loved me and was really willing to forgive me for my sins. I became convinced during a trip to West Lafayette, Indiana, that without God my life had no meaning, no joy, and no hope of life beyond the grave.

On this trip a friend talked with me for hours about the gospel of Christ. I remember those hours as clearly as if they had occurred yesterday. My sinfulness distressed me. I felt lost. I doubted my worth. My friend patiently took the time to show me important truths from the Bible, especially from Romans 5 and 6.

Slowly God's love started to feel warm around my cold soul. I began to believe that Christ died for my sins, just as the Bible says. I became absolutely certain that Jesus *is* the Christ, the Son of God and my Savior and Lord. I felt an urgency to claim him and obtain forgiveness of all my sins.

Like those on the day of Pentecost who became convinced that Jesus was the promised Savior I cried out, "What must I do to be saved?" Then my friend told me to turn my heart toward God and be baptized into Christ, and God would make me totally clean from the past, give me a new life, and provide his Spirit as a gift to live in me.

We went to a place with water and I was immersed into Christ, trusting only in the cleaning power of the blood of Jesus Christ for my salvation. The joy I experienced as I laid my burdened past down and rose up from that water was thrilling and yet at the same time the calmest moment I had ever experienced. I felt I had great value to God because of what he had done in my soul.

I made a promise that night to seek him, to love and serve him. That promise has given direction to my life every day since then. I've fallen down and failed a lot but God always helps me up.

I am a Christian—nothing more, nothing less, and it's all because of God's incredible kindness and grace in my life. I plan to die as a Christian, one who seeks to love God and love my neighbor to the best of my ability. I will not quit.

I'll never apologize for my faith; instead, I'll try to live it in such a way that others will think well of my God. I'll try to courageously speak the truth in love whenever God provides the opportunity for me to help another person understand his love.

I always try to lovingly persuade people rather than order them around. Each person, believer and unbeliever, has dignity before God and is free to choose him and his ways—or not. I believe each one of us has a soul and a God-shaped vacuum that only he can fill if we are to be happy and defeat death. Jesus is Lord, and one day everyone will say it is true. Until that day, each can decide God's place in his or her life.

My life has been richly blessed. The finest person I've ever known is my loving wife, Camilla. God has given us four unique, gifted, and loving children, who have taught us much about God.

I had two serious bouts with cancer, one in 1973–74 and the second in 1981–82. Only by the grace of God am I alive today—I really mean it, for I almost died. I understand very personally that each day is a gift of God.

In all the dark nights I have never been alone or abandoned by God (although I've felt that way sometimes). Maybe cancer has been my "thorn in the flesh" (2 Cor. 12). Yet even so, I have been given incredible love and strength by my heavenly Father and I must praise him at every opportunity.

A professor of mine once wrote a line that I have made my own: "The miracle is in your hope, not in your healing." Without doubt, God has physically healed me from cancer, not *once* but *twice*. I believe in the powerful God who answers prayer! He brought me from death to life, and that is wonderful.

But there is something far more wonderful. Because God allowed Jesus to go to the cross for all of us, and because he raised him from the dead, you and I have a *hope* that is the great miracle. Even though one day I will die, I look forward to life beyond the grave with God and all those in his family, the church of Jesus Christ. The best miracle is that my soul has been healed.

You can understand why I'm a happy man, can't you? Even with constant troubles and trials I know God holds my future in his hand. That future is bright because of what he has done and what he has promised. That's why I love him.

My prayer for you is that your testimony, different from mine, ends at the same place—Jesus Christ. Be sure you are in him. What an amazing grace he has given you and me.

Training Opportunities

Because an evangelistic lifestyle is a way of thinking, speaking, and serving people, it requires training. Enjoyable, affordable tools and training opportunities exist. There are features of each program that may not fit your personality and style but they can develop in you an "outreach mind-set" and a comfort zone for verbalizing your faith to outsiders. That's our goal. Most believers have had little training in communicating the gospel to the uncommitted.

The finest resource I know for showing you how to tell your story of what God has done, with excellent examples, is Leighton Ford's *The Power of Story.* Ford says of his book:

> It is written to encourage the average layperson to tell his or her own story, and in the process, to help spread the story of God. . . . If you have become a part of the story of God, then you have a story to share with the people around you.[2]

Alistair McGrath's *Explaining Your Faith without Losing Your Friends* lays out the various ways Scripture describes salvation. One program that has trained thousands is Evangelism Explosion, a program of the Coral Ridge Church in Fort Lauderdale, Florida. The total emphasis is on training nonspecialists—everyday Christian believers.

Bill Hybels and Mark Mittelberg in their book on relational evangelism, *Becoming a Contagious Christian,* show natural everyday activities being done to effectively communicate the faith of Jesus Christ.[3] Mark Mittlelberg is the primary author of *The Contagious Christian Training Course,* a curriculum designed to build skills and confidence in the area of relational evangelism. The material is designed for a small group of six to eight, specifically for everyday believers who are convinced that evangelism is *not* their area. This material helps us see we can spiritually impact the people we know in ways that are natural to our personalities. I find outstanding and practical their suggestions on ways to build relationships with non-Christians and to talk meaningfully with them. The course comes with video vignettes, leader's manual, and participant guides.

Ben Johnson has spent years training Christians for real-world evangelism. He has developed an excellent resource for evangelism, *Friend-Maker for God,* a faith-sharing seminar that teaches a simple, nonthreatening method for sharing faith in daily life. The audio/video/print packet is designed for thirteen sessions of forty minutes each.[4] Also, the sixteen-hour video series *Caring Evangelism: How to Live and Share Christ's Love* is excellent for training everyday Christians who have yet to receive practical equipping for outreach.[5]

The Navigators in Colorado Springs develop impressive resources for evangelism, including print resources that are attractive evangelistic tools. Recently the paperback *The Power of Hope,* the gospel story from a translation by Eugene Peterson, has become available. Also their monthly magazine, *Discipleship,* frequently includes useful articles for impacting the lives around you for Christ.[6]

Richard Peace has revised his widely used *Small Group Evangelism,* adding a study guide for training groups.

Hands-on training opportunities, usually one-week seminars, are offered by The Cove in Montreat, North Carolina, and Campus Crusade in Colorado Springs.[7] These training opportunities are moderately priced and are geared to training the participant to return to a local congregation with skills to train lay Christians for evangelism.

Walter Brueggemann says that when Christians tell what God has done and show evidence by their transformed lives, they participate in the same work of God as those in the Book of Acts did. What greater honor could we have than to take our place in the long line of those who have faithfully told the same story of the redemptive action of God through the birth, life, death, and resurrection of Jesus?[8]

9

The Use
of Mass Media

Perhaps then it is only working with those in need
that we will be able to help them articulate their first
cry of help to God.

William Dyrness

Mass media evangelism is controversial. Friends in
graduate school pointed me to Malcolm Muggeridge's book
Christ and Media and warned that the media distorts the
message, especially when speakers soft-pedal the demands
of discipleship while highlighting the benefits of "being
saved." Respected ministers urged me to accept that Herald
of Truth had no hope of "connecting with the culture." The
ministry was hopelessly tied to the past—a prisoner of past

98

methods—and therefore would be ineffective. They made some points worthy of careful study. Later, many signaled the death of mass media evangelistic outreach with the televangelist scandals of the '80s.

Yet it was hard to live in the mailbag, like I did, and ignore the earnest longings of people to make sense out of their lives. They wanted help. They desired reasons for hope. They sought faith. They wanted to know if there is a personal God who loves them and cares what happens to them.

These respondents were willing to study the Bible—if we would help them know how to start. Some were willing to implement the solutions found in the gospel—especially if there were Christians near with whom they could share the struggle. Seeing lives turned around and people in whom God's love begins to work makes me appreciate the communication process that facilitated those changes.

My work with the Herald of Truth Media Ministries over the last twenty-six years causes me to believe broadcast and print media remain powerful avenues to touch people's lives. The recent CBS television series *Christy* is evidence that programming emphasizing Christian values can be enjoyed by a mass audience who have the opportunity to witness the positive aspects of a Christian worldview. The PBS series, hosted by Bill Moyers, that told the story of the gospel hymn "Amazing Grace" gave millions an opportunity to overhear the gospel story without attending church. The powerful transformation of John Newton from slave owner to Christian is as powerful a gospel sermon as many will ever hear.

Herald of Truth has produced and aired four television specials from New York and Washington, D.C., which have given viewers an opportunity to see the spiritual foundations of our country and have invited them to consider a new spiritual beginning for themselves. More than twenty-five thousand responded requesting further information.

Michael Horton writes that the loss of community and the upheaval in dependable values help make Americans feel off-balance when considering what really can be counted on in the future. With that uncertainty comes a willingness on the part of many to listen.[1] A credible, caring voice for God can still receive a hearing. People want to investigate for themselves.

A number of people disagree with me that mass media can be a valid way to discuss the gospel. But Leander Keck, himself somewhat skeptical, writes, "It is not too late . . . to do something positive in communicating through TV." Keck recommends programs on commercial TV stations that tell about "ordinary people's efforts to be faithful Christians." He says that the reason network TV "can never be a truly proper means of evangelism [is because] it cannot connect people with a real community of faith, a local church." He believes that what TV does best is "arouse curiosity about and cultivate a positive disposition toward Christianity."[2]

For years Herald of Truth Ministries has considered response follow-up and linkage with local churches near the respondent (where possible and appropriate) a vital part of the broadcast process. Many have begun the road to faith and commitment to Christ through our radio, TV, and print efforts. The keys to success remain:

- the responsible use of the medium
- the integrity of the broadcaster and message
- having little or no on-air fundraising

- linkage with a caring local community of Christians for follow-up teaching and ministry

Radio speaker Glenn Owen combined daily radio Bible teaching with seminars in the cities of his listeners. He had strong local church involvement, and the result was that people came to Christ.

I've served as editor of *UpReach* magazine for eight years. The magazine is designed as a tool for Christians to use with their non-Christian friends, showing how faith in Christ makes a difference in everyday life. Reports continue to come in that the magazine is effective as a part of the evangelistic process. It's true that much religious broadcasting is reinforcement or faith-confirming for the already believing Christian—but not all. Christians should use the tools they believe will help them impact people for Christ.

Our Mexico evangelist, Lou Seckler, has successfully combined daily radio programs, weekly television programs, and local evangelistic campaigns for more than twenty years in the Mexico Harvest campaign. God has blessed these efforts with the establishment of forty-five churches across Mexico. When mass media is a strong part of an overall strategic evangelistic outreach it can be a powerful tool for God's purposes. When used for empire building or other self-serving goals it will hurt the evangelistic mission of Christians.

John White has written a devastating rebuke of "evangelism abuse" that anyone working in mass media broadcasting should read and reflect on. John bluntly rejects any manipulation used to produce conversions. We should never make people anxious, induce guilt, or bypass their rational judgment.[3] This is my problem with those who like the approach, "If you should die tonight, why should God let you into his heaven?" I wonder sometimes if we overstep our place in God's process. Do we have confidence that the Holy Spirit will convict a person of sin? We must never seek to win converts in ways that violate the gospel. We need to trust that God is working even when we cannot see the results. Contrary to popular opinion, we evangelists are not in sales. People come to Christ by his Spirit and power, not our airtight arguments or emotional appeals. Our desire to be a human instrument God can and will use is very good. But again, we don't drag people into the kingdom—they walk in wanting to come for all the right reasons. Let's remember the work of evangelism is God's work and he is patient. Changing hearts requires God's Spirit working through the faithful telling of the story. We don't have to be manipulative.

Some will suggest I'm ignoring the need to "close the sale"—get a response and commitment from someone for Christ. Not at all. Yes, there is a time to ask someone if they want to make a decision. But some methods smack of selling shoes, not inviting a person to decide they want God to rule their life. In all our evangelistic efforts, including the use of mass media, we Christians represent Christ and must be beyond reproach.

How do you fit into this scenario? Can everyday Christians use mass media for evangelism? No one who knows me is surprised when I suggest that everyday Christians have opportunities to be involved in mass media. The evidence comes from the ways Christians are using our weekly thirty-minute program *Hope for Life's Journey.* Some are placing the program on public access channels. In some instances, congregations are buying station time for these weekly broadcasts. Individuals are also purchasing single programs for one-time broadcast in smaller TV markets across our country. And home Bible study groups are using the programs as the basis for monthly neighborhood Bible study fellowships. Christians are using media to tell others about Christ.

10

Ready to Serve

We must not suppose that *we* could convert anyone.
God is sovereign in salvation: He alone can take the
scales from people's eyes; by his Spirit alone does the
work of regeneration—new birth—begin.

Alan Sell

I believe we can be powerful tools in God's hand to
impact our family, friends, and associates with the gospel
of Jesus Christ. We must first develop the heart that desires
to bring God the honor and glory he deserves. Then we
must cultivate a vision of people that corresponds to his
love for them. Then we must pray to develop ways of thinking, living, and speaking that I describe as service with a
heart toward reconciliation.

Once we have done these things and so have a "strong
consciousness of being God's peculiar people" we should
plan with other Christians ways to be God's agents of reconciliation in our corner of the world.[1]

The plan may be similar to what the Korean church is doing. It could begin with a time of prayer among six to eight Christians and the decision to meet once a month to utilize Mark Mittelberg's *Contagious Christian Training Course.* Then you may make a list of people you desire to impact for God. So we don't become overwhelmed by the size of the task, Lee Strobel suggests:

> Start where you are. Think of three specific irreligious people in your own life—not a mass of faceless skeptics but three individuals within your sphere of influence. People you can pray for. People you can deepen your relationship with. People you can share your faith with over time. People you can invite to seeker-oriented events. Make them your personal mission field.[2]

Prayer is vital. Without a time of focused prayer, for ourselves and those we seek to influence, we will be frustrated and erratic.

I have a personal evangelistic plan listing those in my family, two people with whom I work, six of my neighbors, and five acquaintances with whom I serve on boards in community activities. I pray for them by name and seek to serve them in any crisis area they or their family may encounter. Included on my list are three single parents, two retired military personnel, one atheist, and two who are openly agnostic. My list totals fifteen whom I specifically pray and interact with plus any other acquaintances and one-time encounters whom God may use. As I've said, we do not know everything God may be doing through us.

Everyday evangelism cannot be done on the scale of success or failure. We are all failures in that we are broken people. Look at our families. Review for a moment with me the Bible picture of brokenness. Where is the perfect family in Scripture?

A search of Scripture turns up one rather surprising truth: There are no exemplary families. Not a single family is portrayed in Scripture in such a way as to evoke admiration. There are many family stories, there is considerable reference to family life, and there is sound counsel to guide the growth of families, but not a single model family for anyone to look up to in either awe or envy.

Adam and Eve are no sooner out of the garden than their children get into a fight. Shem and Japheth are forced to devise a strategy to hide their father's drunken shame. Jacob and Esau are bitter rivals and sow seeds of discord that bear centuries of bitter harvest. Joseph and his brothers bring variations on the themes of sibling rivalry and parental bungling. Jesse's sons, brave and loyal in service of their country, are capricious and cruel to their youngest brother. David is unfortunate in both wives and children—he is a man after God's own heart and Israel's greatest king, but he cannot manage his own household.

Even in the family of Jesus, where we might expect something different, there is the same theme. The picture in Mark 3 strikes us as typical rather than exceptional. Jesus is active, healing the sick, comforting the distressed, and fulfilling his calling as Messiah, while his mother and brothers are outside trying to get him to come home, quite sure that he is crazy. Jesus' family criticizes and does not appreciate him.

We are faced daily with the reality that something has gone wrong with our families. Our children fight and quarrel; our parenting misfires. We are involved in failure and we feel guilty. At the very least, these biblical examples show that no one needs to carry a burden of guilt because his or her family is deficient in qualities that Christian families are supposed to exhibit. More than that, we see that God can use even sinful people to do his work. He forgives them and helps them in their service of him, even though he often lets them suffer the consequences of their sin.

We're calling everyone to God, not to ourselves. We don't have to grade ourselves on how good we are at this work. Our goal is to faithfully keep on offering our lives for the Master's use. I'm convinced such grading leads many to give up evangelistic outreach to those "more gifted" (better at it). Alistair McGrath encourages us this way:

> So if you feel inadequate—don't worry. All of us are inadequate. And by recognizing your inadequacy, you will be all the more likely to trust in God, and not yourself. By recognizing our weakness and lack of wisdom, we turn to God, in order to receive his strength and wisdom. God uses us—but, in the end, he doesn't depend on us . . . it is by claiming his power and presence, and by pointing people to him, that we best serve him.[3]

Will we face times of discouragement? Surely. To know that the living God will "transmit that saving presence to another person through us also made Paul express his feelings of inadequacy."[4] Just remember this: God will bring himself glory through your life. When you follow his leading, there will be persons who were impacted for God because you lived.

Henri Nouwen, in *Life of the Beloved,* puts it this way:

> That our few years on this earth are part of a much larger event that stretches out beyond the boundaries of our birth and death. I think of it as a mission into time, a mission that is very exhilarating, and even exciting, mostly because the One who sent me on the mission is waiting for me to come home and tell the story of what I have learned.[5]

What would our world be like without the story of God's passionate love for us? It would be a world where, as Victor Hugo said, "men are all under sentence of death with an indefinite reprieve." God's story tells us, "The wages of sin is death, but the gift of God is eternal life in Christ Jesus our Lord" (Rom. 6:23). Because we know such news of hope, "each one of us must be a teller of the Story . . . a piece of good news for those we meet."[6]

In the movie *Chariots of Fire* the Olympic runner Eric Liddell, when asked why he raced, replied, "When I run, I feel his pleasure." When you and I seek to reconcile lost people to God through Jesus Christ, we too will "feel his pleasure." We will feel God's pleasure because we will be doing what he wants us to do, what he has commanded us to do. This may not always be easy.

While most books on witnessing or evangelism include a chapter on handling rejection or minimizing the possibility of embarrassment, we may still not be prepared for the rejection that is to come. More and more in America, the Christian faith is being ridiculed as narrow-minded, bigoted, homophobic, simple-minded, and antiscientific. Perhaps we've known little about the offense of the cross up until now because Christians have been respected in our culture. Not so anymore. Chapters in books like *Taking the Fear Out of Evangelism* that suggest, "we can witness and invite in ways they will welcome instead of rejecting"[7] may have to be revised as we enter the twenty-first century. No one desires the reputation of "fanatic," nor does any lover of God want his actions or words to alienate people. But if we don't speak and act we don't belong to him (Matt. 10:32). And if what we must say about Jesus is offensive to our hearers, we must expect rejection and even ridicule.

In the future we'll need God's Spirit and each other more than ever. We will have to come closer to our Lord. We will need to constantly refer to 1 Peter and to Christian books that tie our times to those of the first Christians.[8] However, we have no need to fear; God is the sovereign Lord over his universe, and his victory is sure. As Paul wrote in Philippians 2:10–11, "Every knee should bow . . . and every tongue confess that Jesus Christ is Lord, to the glory of God the Father." Until then, we will become more acquainted with real spiritual warfare, and we'll fully use the weapons God provides for us.

We are involved in God's great purpose. In his final earthly appearance to the disciples in Jerusalem Jesus said, "You will receive power when the Holy Spirit comes on you; and you shall be my witnesses in Jerusalem, and in all Judea and Samaria, and to the ends of the earth" (Acts 1:10).

There's no question that God's desire is for all to come to a knowledge of the truth about what he has done in Christ, for he desires "all men to be saved." I'm proposing that all of us are involved in God's ministry of evangelism, perhaps in different ways and styles, but the Christian's heart is a heart of reconciliation, so every Christian desires his or her life to speak to others of God's goodness.

It's true that God alone can turn sinners from their sin and bring them to everlasting life. My appeal to you is that you, in constant dependence on his Spirit, let him use you for his glory to touch other lives for Christ. If you will do this, you can say with Paul the apostle, "We are laborers together with God" (1 Cor. 3:9), and one day our Lord will say to us, "Well done, good and faithful servant."

Discussion Guide

Chapter 1 *Telling the Story*

1. "Our *real* story is how our stories have met with God's redemption story" (p. 25). How has being saved by Jesus Christ impacted your life? What are some ways you can use your personal encounter with Christ to tell those around you of the difference he can make in their lives? If you have a difficult time speaking to others about Christ, are there ways you can communicate your salvation story in writing (such as letters to old friends, an article for a magazine or newsletter, or witnessing to people on the Internet)?

2. "Lost people are captured by many lies. They live under the dominion of the enemy" (p. 26). How can the truth that the lost are in bondage to Satan change your view of and response to the unsaved around you?

3. Recall a time when you shared your faith with a lost person who didn't respond to the gospel. How did this experience affect your passion for evangelism? What are some ways in which your perspective on one-on-one evangelism has changed since that experience?

4. What has your experience been with "service evangelism"? How can we love people through acts of unconditional kindness while still maintaining an evangelistic edge?

5. "God's initiative *precedes* our response. . . . When we tell the story, God has already been at work before we arrive" (p. 32). How does this concept of the sovereign God drawing people to himself impact your view of evangelism? What are some ways you have used this truth as an excuse to be silent about your faith?

Chapter 2 *A Passion for Evangelism*

1. When first coming to Christ, people are often very zealous for reaching the lost, but after time such passion may fade. How would you rate your current passion for reaching lost people? If your zeal has faded, why has it? What would it take for God to rekindle a fire in your heart for telling the story of Christ to others?

2. "Nothing brings us greater satisfaction than to testify about the love of God" (p. 34). Who in your web of influence especially needs a tangible expression of the love of God? What are some specific ways you can be used by the Lord to share Christ's love to this hurting person?

3. Being a witness "means we have seen and heard something (namely the love of God in Christ) that has totally changed our life and so we are willing to tell about it" (p. 35). Describe the difference between being a witness for Christ and just telling people facts about Christ and the gospel. Tell of a time when your changed life led others to follow Christ.

4. How does gratitude for God's grace in your life impact your involvement in serving others and sharing Christ with them?

5. What are some of the greatest challenges to being an evangelist every day—on the job, with friends, with family members? What are some of the greatest opportunities for being a Christian witness in your everyday life?

6. The early church was obviously very evangelistic. A reading of Acts reveals the driving force of their zeal—they were empowered by the Holy Spirit. In what ways are you leaning on the Holy Spirit each day for courage to witness to and love the lost? What are some specific areas of your life that need transformation by the Holy Spirit to make you a brighter light before the world's darkness (your tongue, your character, your integrity)?

Chapter 3 *The World We Live In*

1. What are some signs you see around you that America is a "post-Christian" country? How can this increasing secularization be turned into opportunities for sharing Christ with others?

2. What are some of your greatest fears in sharing the gospel with secular people?

3. Too often Christians have seen evangelism as merely telling people the truth of the gospel. How would listening first to an unbeliever's story and worldview open up possibilities for their listening to the Good News?

4. "In caring evangelism people are free to respond to the story and are not argued into the kingdom of God" (p. 44). In what ways have you seen a caring approach to evangelism serve as an effective approach? Identify some populations in your community who may be overlooked (homeless, single moms, unemployed). How can you and your church begin a caring evangelism ministry to such people who hunger for compassion?

5. In a world devoid of much objective truth, how can we present to modern man the truth of Jesus Christ, his death, and resurrection?

6. Read Paul's address at the meeting of the Areopagus in Acts 17:22–31. He was addressing people who had never heard the gospel. How can Paul's methods of presenting the gospel to the pagan world be applied to our interaction with those in today's secular culture?

7. What are some of the unique challenges of communicating the gospel to secular people who have a Christian background of some type (such as those raised with a nominal affiliation to a church)?

8. Idolatry was a common sin among those in the culture to whom the early church proclaimed Jesus. What are some of the "idols" of today's world? How does the message of Jesus Christ speak to the void in the lives of people who are caught up in contemporary idolatry?

Chapter 4 *Ordinary Christian Evangelists*

1. Who are the Nellie Moreheads of your life—the people who quietly go about the work of serving and giving to oth-

ers and of telling anyone interested about Jesus? How could you do the same?

2. Lee Strobel said that his memory of his life before Christ motivates him to help bring others into God's family (see p. 48). Think for a moment what your life and future would be without the Lord. Name someone you know who is still living a life of irrelevancy without Christ. What are some ways you can point him or her to the living Christ?

3. It is through the web of their relationships that most people become Christians today. Who were some of the main people who influenced you to give your life to Christ? Who are some nonbelievers in your web of relationships with whom you can have the greatest Christian influence?

4. Read Colossians 4:2–6. What are some specific ways you can put this Scripture into practice with those close to you? Write them down and pray about them. Find at least one Christian friend with whom you can pray and live out what Paul says.

5. What do you find to be the greatest frustration in being an "ordinary Christian evangelist"? Explain your answer.

6. What have you discovered to be the greatest freedom and joy in carrying out the ministry of everyday evangelism? Explain your answer.

7. In 1 Thessalonians 2:8 the apostle Paul tells the church, "We loved you so much that we were delighted to share with you not only the gospel of God but our lives as well." What are some creative ways you can share your life with those you

are trying to reach with the gospel? These could include working with someone on a project, involvement in the community, or recreation activities.

Chapter 5 *Opportunities for Evangelism*

1. Discuss the evangelistic styles. Which one have you seen most often? Which one do you prefer to use?

2. William Dyrness believes that the experiences people go through may make them more responsive to hearing the gospel (see p. 59). Share any situations you've experienced where persons became open to considering the gospel message because of what they were going through.

3. Steve Sjogren's "Conspiracy of Kindness" suggests that Christians participate in the process of evangelism by meeting the real needs of people. Do you believe he is right? Give examples.

4. Discuss the small group model for evangelism described by Dennis Guernsey (pp. 62–63). Do you believe it offers possibilities for God to use you in evangelistic outreach to someone in your friendship circle? How?

5. How do Christians avoid manipulation when they, with a heart for evangelism, serve people in crisis? What is required for you to allow people to freely accept or reject Jesus?

6. In America today do you believe it's beneficial to non-Christians to invite them to a church worship service? Give your reasons.

7. Discuss the possibilities for speaking about Jesus in the workplace. What cautions do you believe should be considered?

Chapter 6 *Special Arenas for Evangelism*

1. The gospel is for the "poor" and the "rich." How could you begin to connect with those who are materially wealthy but may be impoverished in their souls?

2. Discuss Jesus' interaction with the rich young man (Matt. 19:16–22). What do you learn from Jesus that will help you influence the rich?

3. Loving those in need of food and clothing by supplying their needs honors God. In what ways can words of witness be given to them?

4. Kent Amos utilized his house and his children's social network to influence young people. Discuss ways to utilize your home and family friendships to influence people for Christ.

5. In what ways does your family practice inclusion and work on being "redemptive" with those who share meals with you?

Chapter 7 *The Role of Your Church*

1. Discuss the climate for evangelism in the church where you worship. Are you eager or reluctant to invite your friends who are not Christians to attend?

2. In your experience what do "seekers" and those whose lives are in crisis look for when they attend church?

3. Do you agree with Jack Hayford's observations about the role of worship in evangelism (see p. 84)?

4. Should churches do more to explain the church service to outsiders who may be attending for the first time? If so, what would you recommend?

5. Read chapters 2–8 of Acts and discuss why you believe the Christian message was well received by many who heard it in the earliest days of the church's existence.

Chapter 8 *Training for Telling Your Story*

1. In 2 Corinthians 5:18–21 Paul states that God has given us the message and ministry of reconciliation. Describe what this means for lay Christians (those who are not ministers).

2. In what ways has your story of God's grace to you found a place in your conversations on the days between Sundays?

3. Write down your story of conversion. In your group take turns reading these stories. Discuss ways your story could be shared verbally in other settings.

4. Discuss having an evangelism training experience for developing greater skills for sharing faith with those who do not know God's love. Seek to formulate a specific program sometime in the next six months and covenant together to do it.

5. Discuss ways to communicate to children in your group the gospel story of redemption. Decide on a plan for reaching out to children that will be utilized in the next six months.

Chapter 9 *The Use of Mass Media*

1. Discuss your impressions of religious teaching on radio and TV. Share positive and negative impressions you've personally experienced.

2. What damage to your faith has occurred because of excesses or scandals involving mass media evangelists?

3. Can the mass media be utilized in any valid way to communicate hope in Jesus Christ? If so, how?

4. Are there positive ways to use print or electronic media for spreading the gospel where you live? Discuss ways your group could make use of mass media in evangelism.

5. How can you feel confident that the time has come to ask a friend to surrender his or her life to Jesus Christ as Lord and accept him as Savior? What indicators should be present before you ask?

6. Discuss ways to assure that you aren't being manipulative in your relationship with someone. How can you be sure when you are witnessing that you're trusting in the power of the gospel and not your persuasive techniques?

Chapter 10 *Ready to Serve*

1. This chapter emphasizes the need to remember we're all broken people in need of redemption. How will this emphasis aid evangelistic outreach?

2. Make a list of three people you want to see God bring to himself—using your life as an instrument of influence—and tell the group about these people so they can join you in prayer for them.

3. List suggestions your group gives you for making the most of your opportunities to serve these people in the name of Christ.

4. How are we colaborers with God in evangelism?

5. Since evangelism is a way of seeing the world through God's eyes, discuss how we can increase our awareness of evangelistic opportunities.

6. Do you believe that in the near future Christians in America will encounter increasing resistance and opposition as we witness to our faith in Jesus as Savior and Lord? What effects will increased resistance to evangelism have on Christians?

7. Have you ever suffered ridicule for taking a stand for Christ and the truths of the Bible? Share experiences with others in the group.

8. Picture the final judgment. What images come to your mind? In what ways do these images deepen your sense of urgency to share Christ with those in your circle of influence?

Notes

Preface: *As We Begin*

1. David J. Gyertson, ed., *Salt and Light: A Christian Response to Current Issues* (Dallas: Word, 1993), 12.

Chapter 1: *Telling the Story*

1. *Life* (December 1994), 68.
2. Ibid.
3. William H. Willimon, *The Intrusive Word* (Grand Rapids: Eerdmans, 1994), 5.
4. Leighton Ford, *The Power of Story* (Colorado Springs: NavPress, 1994), 77.
5. Willimon, *The Intrusive Word,* 5.
6. This is discussed fully by David S. Dockery in "A Theological Foundation for Evangelism" in *Evangelism in the Twenty-First Century,* ed. Thom S. Rainer (Wheaton: Harold Shaw, 1989), 77–87.
7. Bill Bright, "Personal Evangelism: Conquering the Fear of Failure" in *Evangelism in the Twenty-First Century,* ed. Rainer, 156.
8. Steve Sjogren, *Conspiracy of Kindness* (Ann Arbor, Mich.: Vine Books), 22.

9. Quoted in Robert E. Logan and Larry Short, *Mobilizing for Compassion: Moving People into Ministry* (Grand Rapids: Revell, 1994), 29.

10. William J. Abraham, *The Logic of Evangelism* (Grand Rapids: Eerdmans, 1989), 95.

Chapter 2: *A Passion for Evangelism*

1. Quoted in Earl G. Hunt Jr., *Evangelism for a New Century* (Nashville: Discipleship Resources, 1994), 7.
2. Ibid., 35.
3. Ibid., 35–36.
4. Michael Green, *Evangelism through the Local Church* (Nashville: Oliver Nelson, 1992), 8–9, 11.
5. William H. Willimon, *Why I Am a United Methodist* (Nashville: Abingdon Press, 1990), 119–20.
6. Ibid., 110.
7. Willimon, *The Intrusive Word*, 33–34.

Chapter 3: *The World We Live In*

1. Quoted in Green, *Evangelism through the Local Church*, 261.
2. Charles Colson, "The Naked Public Square," in Gyertson, *Salt and Light*, 275.
3. Myron Augsburger, Calvin Ratz, and Frank Tillapaugh, *Mastering Outreach and Evangelism* (Portland: Multnomah Press, 1990), 17.
4. John Bright, *The Kingdom of God* (Nashville: Abingdon, 1961), 18.
5. Hervé Carrier, S.J., *Evangelizing the Culture of Modernity* (Maryknoll, N.Y.: Orbis, 1993), 1.
6. Ibid., 30.

7. George G. Hunter III, *How to Reach Secular People* (Nashville: Abingdon Press, 1992). Also helpful is Thom and Marcia Hopler, *Reaching the World Next Door* (Downers Grove, Ill.: InterVarsity, 1993). This book is especially good on reaching the Black culture.

8. Green, *Evangelism through the Local Church*, 114–46. Also, I was helped in understanding worldviews by James Sire, *The Universe Next Door* (Downers Grove, Ill.: InterVarsity, 1962).

9. Ronald W. Johnson, *How Will They Hear if We Don't Listen?* (Nashville: Broadman and Holman, 1994), ix. See also "The Power of a Listening Heart" in Logan and Short, *Mobilizing for Compassion*.

10. Willimon, *The Intrusive Word*, 130.

11. William J. McKay, *Me, an Evangelist? Every Christian's Guide to Caring Evangelism* (St. Louis: Stephen Ministries, 1992), 12.

Chapter 4: *Ordinary Christian Evangelists*

1. Rainer, ed. *Evangelism in the Twenty-First Century*, 209.

2. Lee Strobel, *Inside the Mind of Unchurched Harry and Mary* (Grand Rapids: Zondervan, 1993), 98, 102. *Inside the Mind* is now available on audiotape.

3. Jim Nelson Black, *When Nations Die* (Wheaton: Tyndale, 1994), 233.

4. Joseph C. Aldrich, *Gentle Persuasion: Creative Ways to Introduce Your Friends to Christ* (Portland: Multnomah, 1988), 131.

5. George G. Hunter III, *Church Growth: State of the Art* (Wheaton: Tyndale, 1986), 80. See also Hunter, *The Contagious Congregation* (Nashville: Abingdon Press, 1985).

6. Win Arn, *The Master's Plan for Making Disciples* (Eugene, Ore.: Harvest House, 1987), 75, 43.

7. Lyle E. Schaller, *Growing Plans: Six Targets for Growth* (Nashville: Abingdon Press, 1994), 43.

Chapter 5: *Opportunities for Evangelism*

1. Bill Hybels, *Honest to God?* (Grand Rapids: Zondervan, 1990), 120.

2. Ibid., 130.

3. William A. Dyrness, *How Does America Hear the Gospel?* (Grand Rapids: Eerdmans, 1989), 100–101.

4. Ibid., 143–53.

5. J. I. Packer, *The Word of the Cross: A Contemporary Theology of Evangelism,* ed., Lewis A. Drummond (Nashville: Broadman and Holman, 1992).

6. Peter Kreeft, *The God Who Loves You* (Ann Arbor, Mich.: Servant Publications, 1988), 39–40.

7. Steve Sjogren, *Conspiracy of Kindness,* 131.

8. Ibid., 135, 238, 120–24.

9. Richard Peace, *Small Group Evangelism: A Training Program for Reaching Out with the Gospel* (Downers Grove, Ill.: InterVarsity, 1985).

10. Frank Pittman, *Turning Points: Treating Families in Transition and Crisis* (New York: Guilford Press, 1989), 17.

11. Bruce Powers, *Growing Faith: How It Develops and How It Can Be Nurtured* (Nashville: Broadman and Holman, 1982).

A good resource for understanding the stages in the family life cycle is *The Changing Family Life Cycle: A Framework for Family Therapy,* ed., Betty Carter and Monica McGoldrick (New York: Gardner Press, 1990).

12. McKay, *Me, an Evangelist?* 105.

13. David Bosch, *Transforming Mission: Paradigm Shifts in Theology of Mission* (Maryknoll, N.Y.: Orbis Books, 1991), 417.

Chapter 6: *Special Arenas for Evangelism*

1. To understand the world of the affluent, see William Willimon, *The Gospel for the Person Who Has Everything* (Valley Forge, Pa.: Judson Press, 1978). This excellent resource provides special insight into how the rich will hear the gospel.

2. Walter Brueggemann, *Biblical Perspectives on Evangelism* (Nashville: Abingdon Press, 1993), 127.

3. Leonard Allen, *The Cruciform Church* (Abilene, Tex.: ACV Press, 1992).

4. Aldrich, *Gentle Persuasion,* 136. To get started in home evangelism, read the practical pamphlet by Bob and Betty Jacks with Ron Wormser Sr., *Your Home a Lighthouse: Hosting an Evangelistic Bible Study* (Colorado Springs: NavPress, 1986). See also Peter Scazzero, *Introducing Jesus: Starting an Investigative Bible Study for Seekers* (Downers Grove, Ill.: Inter-Varsity Press, 1991).

5. Laura Nash, *Believers in Business* (Nashville: Thomas Nelson, 1994).

6. Ibid., 254.

7. Ibid., 255.

Chapter 7: *The Role of Your Church*

1. Ed Dobson, *Starting a Seeker-Sensitive Service: How Traditional Churches Can Reach the Unchurched* (Grand Rapids: Zondervan, 1993), 7. See also Wade Clark Roof, *A Generation of Seekers: The Spiritual Journeys of the Baby Boom Generation* (New York: Harper and Row, 1993).

2. Alan Sell, *Aspects of Christian Integrity* (Louisville: Westminster/John Knox, 1990), 118.

3. Gareth Icenogle, *Bible Foundations for Small Group Ministry* (Downers Grove, Ill.: InterVarsity, 1994), 352.

4. Bosch, *Transforming Mission,* 414.

5. William Dyrness, *Let the Earth Rejoice* (Westchester, Ill.: Crossway, 1983), 193–94.

6. Jack Hayford, *The Heart of Praise* (Ventura, Calif.: Regal, 1992), 114.

7. Abraham, *The Logic of Evangelism,* 101.

8. André Resner, "Worship or Evangelize," *Restoration Quarterly* (October 1994), 78.

Chapter 8: *Training for Telling Your Story*

1. Alistair McGrath, *Explaining Your Faith without Losing Your Friends* (Grand Rapids: Zondervan, 1989), 69.

2. Ford, *The Power of Story,* 15.

3. Bill Hybels and Mark Mittelberg, *Becoming a Contagious Christian* (Grand Rapids: Zondervan, 1994). I urge every Christian who wants to effectively impact people for Christ to purchase *The Contagious Christian Training Course,* which includes the book and other materials, because of its practicality and wonderful real-life stories. Call 1-800-876-SEEK (7335) or check your local bookstore.

4. See Ben Campbell Johnson, *An Evangelism Primer: Practical Principles for Congregations* (Atlanta: John Knox Press, 1983). This is a book designed for the local church. The materials may be ordered from John Knox Press, 341 Ponce de Leon Ave. NE, Atlanta, GA 30365, 1-800-554-4694.

5. Contact Stephen Ministries, 8016 Dale St., St. Louis, MO 63117, 314-645-5511.

6. The Navigators operate a publishing ministry through NavPress, P.O. Box 35001, Colorado Springs, CO 80935. For a free catalog, call 1-800-366-7788.

7. Contact The Cove at P.O. Box 19223, Asheville, NC 29815; 704-298-2092. The address for Campus Crusade is 100 Sunport Lane, Orlando, FL 32809; 407-826-2000.

8. Brueggemann, *Biblical Perspectives,* 8.

Chapter 9: *The Use of Mass Media*

1. Michael Scott Horton, *Made in America: The Shaping of Modern American Evangelicalism* (Grand Rapids: Baker, 1991).

2. Leander E. Keck, *The Church Confident* (Nashville: Abingdon Press, 1993), 112.

3. John White, *Money Isn't God,* rev. ed. (Downers Grove, Ill.: InterVarsity Press, 1993), 75–89.

Chapter 10: *Ready to Serve*

1. Peace, *Small Group Evangelism,* 225.

2. Strobel, *Inside the Mind,* 224.

3. McGrath, *Explaining Your Faith,* 18–19.

4. Ben Campbell Johnson, *Speaking of God: Evangelism as Initial Spiritual Guidance* (Louisville: Westminster/John Knox, 1991), 162–63.

5. Henri Nouwen, *Life of the Beloved* (New York: Crossroad Publishing, 1992), 180.

6. William A. Barry, *God's Passionate Desire and Our Response* (Notre Dame, Ind.: Ave Maria Press, 1993), 117.

7. William J. McKay, *Taking the Fear Out of Evangelism* (St. Louis: Stephen Ministries, 1992), 12.

8. See Stanley Hauerwas and William Willimon, *Resident Aliens* (Nashville: Abingdon Press, 1989), and James Thompson, *The Church in Exile* (Abilene, Tex.: ACV Press, 1993). Os Guinness explains the causes of our culture wars in *The American Hour* (New York: Macmillan, Free Press, 1993), and James Davison Hunter describes the climate I'm alluding to in *Culture Wars* (New York: Basic Books, 1991).

Further Reading

Barna, George. *Evangelism That Works: How to Reach Changing Generations with the Unchanging Gospel.* Ventura, Calif.: Regal, 1995. George Barna's survey of the beliefs of unchurched people across America helps us understand them as we seek to share the faith of Christ with them. His suggestions for introducing Christ to nonbelievers in the over-thirty Buster generation as a natural part of conversation growing out of relationships with them is especially useful.

Stebbins, Tom. *Friendship Evangelism by The Book.* Camp Hill, Pa.: Christian Publications, 1995. This book explores the biblical perspective for understanding and implementing friendship evangelism. The illustrations and stories demonstrate the power of viewing natural relationships as the focus for evangelism.

Wright, Linda Raney. *Christianity's Crisis in Evangelism: Going Where the People Are.* Gresham, Ore.: Vision House, 1995. This is an outstanding resource for one-on-one evangelism. Wright's audience analysis provides excellent insights into what people value and how they will hear the gospel today.

Randy Becton is director of U.S. programming at Herald of Truth and editor of *UpReach* magazine. He also currently hosts the ministry's daily radio program *A Caring Touch* and the weekly TV program *Hope for Life's Journey.* Becton was recently selected by the government of Israel to serve as a founding member of the Israel Christian Advisory Council, which will advise Israel on strengthening Jewish-Christian relations. He is the author of more than fifteen books.

Herald of Truth began in 1952 and is the largest radio, television, and print evangelism outreach of Churches of Christ in North America. *Caring Touch* is heard daily on 260 radio stations across the United States. *Hope for Life's Journey* is broadcast weekly on several networks as well as on hundreds of independent television stations.

UpReach magazine is a bimonthly inspirational magazine, which has won numerous awards for graphic excellence in Christian journalism.